The Art of
Wyndham Lewis

A. PORTRAIT OF THE ARTIST

THE ART OF
WYNDHAM LEWIS

edited by

CHARLES HANDLEY-READ

*with an essay on detail in the Artist's style,
a chronological outline and notes on the plates*

*With a critical evaluation
by*

ERIC NEWTON

FABER AND FABER LIMITED
24 Russell Square
London

First published in mcmli
by Faber and Faber Limited
24 Russell Square, London, WC1
Printed in Great Britain
by the Shenval Press, London and Hertford

Editor's Acknowledgments

If I have inadvertently omitted acknowledgments where they are due, I hope that an apology here will be accepted. I wish to record my gratitude to the following for help and information supplied to me in the course of preparing this book:

To Mr Martin Baldwin (Director) and the Art Gallery of Toronto, Canada; and to Miss Sibyl Pantazzi, Librarian.

To Mr David Baxandall (Director) and the City Art Gallery, Manchester; also for facilities granted when the block for the Frontispiece was made.

To Mr G. J. V. Bemrose (Curator) and the Public Museum and Art Gallery, Hanley; also for the photograph from which Pl. 42 was made.

To Mr E. C. Chubb (Director) and the Museum and Art Gallery, Durban, South Africa.

To Mr J. W. Goodison (Assistant Director) and the Fitzwilliam Museum, Cambridge.

To Dr T. J. Honeyman (Director) and the Glasgow Art Gallery; also for the photograph from which Pl. 36 was made.

To the Keeper of Pictures, the Imperial War Museum, London; and to Mrs J. D. Oxford-Coxall; also for the photograph from which Pl. 26 was made.

To Mr James Laver (Keeper of the Department of Engraving, Illustration and Design) and the Victoria and Albert Museum, London.

To the Master and Fellows of Magdalene College, Cambridge, for facilities granted when the block for Colour Plate B was made.

To Mr H. O. McCurry (Director) and the National Gallery of Canada, Ottawa.

To Mr Clifford Musgrave (Director) and the Art Gallery and Museum, Brighton.

To Mr Ernest Musgrave (Director) and Temple Newsam House, Leeds.

To Mr A. E. Popham (Keeper of Prints and Drawings) and the British Museum, London.

To Dr John Rothenstein (Keeper) and the Tate Gallery, London; and to the Publications Department; also for the photographs from which Pls. 16, 37 and 47 were made.

To Mr Richard Seddon (Director) and the Graves Art Gallery, Sheffield.

To Mr Munroe Wheeler (Director of Exhibitions and Publications) and the Museum of Modern Art, New York, USA; also for the photograph from which Pl. 15 was made.

I am similarly indebted to the following:

To Mr Osbert H. Barnard and Craddock and Barnard.

To Messrs Brown and Philips and the Leicester Galleries; also for the photographs from which Pls. 18, 19 and 40 were made.

To Mrs Cicely G. Marchant and the Kensington Art Gallery.

To Mr F. H. Mayor and the Mayor Gallery.

To Mr Rex Nan Kivell and the Redfern Gallery; also for the photograph from which Pl. 44 was made; and for numerous facilities granted during the Retrospective Exhibition.

To Messrs A. J. A. McNeill Reid and W. Peploe and the Lefevre Galleries; also for the photograph from which Pl. 17 was made.

To Mr A. Zwemmer and the Zwemmer Gallery.

My thanks are also due to Sir Colin Anderson for facilities granted when the block for Colour Plate C was made.

And I am indebted also to the following friends:

To Alexander Plunket Greene for his assistance in measuring pictures and in helping to record numerous details; to Andrew Wordsworth; to W. E. W. Carpenter-Jacobs who took the excellent photographs from which Pls. 1, 3, 8, 11, 14, 34, 35, 38 and 41 were made; to Kenneth Wood for information supplied to him by Miss Harriet Weaver; to Michael Cartwright Sharp who very kindly assisted with proof-reading; and especially to John P. Harthan of the Victoria and Albert Museum, for much advice and encouragement.

Finally I would like to record my thanks to Mr Eric Newton for his Essay; and to Mr Wyndham Lewis himself for his encouragement, his patience in replying to innumerable questions, and for allowing the use in this publication of many photographs in his possession.

Contents

Illustrations

MONOCHROME PLATES (Continued)

21. THE MUD CLINIC
22. INCA WITH BIRDS
23. FOUR FIGURE COMPOSITION
24. ALLEGRESSE AQUATIQUE
25. WHAT THE SEA IS LIKE AT NIGHT
26. A BATTERY SHELLED
27. RED NUDE
28. GIRL IN A WINDSOR CHAIR
29. GIRL LOOKING DOWN
30. STUDY OF AN ELDERLY MAN
31. WOMAN WITH CLASPED HANDS
32. SEATED FIGURE
33. GIRL SEWING
34. MRS DESMOND HARMSWORTH
35. THE CHAIN SMOKER
36. PORTRAIT OF MRS T. J. HONEYMAN
37. PORTRAIT OF MISS EDITH SITWELL
38. WOMAN IN AN ARMCHAIR
39. PORTRAIT DRAWING OF THE ARTIST'S WIFE
40. PORTRAIT OF T. S. ELIOT
41. THE RED PORTRAIT
42. PORTRAIT OF STEPHEN SPENDER
43. PORTRAIT OF MRS NAOMI MITCHISON
44. PORTRAIT DRAWING OF AVRION, SON OF MRS MITCHISON
45. LYNETTE
46. HEAD OF EZRA POUND (Sketch)
47. PORTRAIT OF EZRA POUND
48. PORTRAIT OF JOHN MACLEOD

Editor's Foreword

The essays in this book accompany selected reproductions representing Wyndham Lewis's work between 1912 and 1950, a period of nearly forty years. While major works have been quoted, and many of them reproduced, it is beyond the scope of this book to provide either a catalogue *raisonné* or a complete history, up to date, of Mr Wyndham Lewis's entire artistic career. The pursuit of material soon revealed (through no fault of the artist) an absence of certain records and the impossibility of obtaining several desirable photographs; and the chief instances of loss, destruction and inaccessibility have been recorded in the Chronological Outline. A number of little-known signed and dated examples of early work survive, notably from the years 1902, 1909 and 1910, and it is acknowledged that the early work of important artists is always of great interest to students. But this book is concerned with Wyndham Lewis's maturity. Therefore the first examples reproduced date from 1912, when the artist was twenty-eight and in full command of his technique. The whole of his work may be grouped in three categories, irrespective of dates:

1. Imaginative Compositions (including the Vorticist examples).

2. Paintings and drawings of the 1914-1918 War.

3. Portraits and drawings from Life.

The reproductions, representing each category, are grouped in this order.

1

Wyndham Lewis

by

ERIC NEWTON

B. PORTRAIT OF T. S. ELIOT (1949)

Wyndham Lewis

Whoever undertakes to write about Mr Wyndham Lewis starts with a heavy handicap. He has to begin where Mr Wyndham Lewis left off. For Mr Wyndham Lewis has himself written copiously about himself and his art, and what he has written cannot be ignored. For he is not only a forceful writer but a clear thinker.

Since I am not a literary critic I dare not say that he writes as well as he paints, but anyone who has read him will know that hard slap in the face that his sentences administer to the reader, the brief, challenging laugh that follows the slap and the sudden note of deadly and often pessimistic seriousness that follows the laugh. Yet, though his writings on art cannot be ignored, they don't quite cover the ground that must be covered in this essay. No sooner does Mr Lewis settle down to define his attitude to art than he becomes distracted by broader issues, and begins to explain what art is, or how it is all but dead, or, well, moribund, or, let's face it, dependent on a crazy world for its chances of recovery. In that vein Mr Lewis is inimitable; he pursues it with such gusto that he forgets his personal artistic problems. Hence this essay. One has no choice but to begin where Mr Lewis left off.

He left off in *Wyndham Lewis the Artist*, published in 1939 and written, characteristically, backwards. It begins with a sort of creed, and it ends with a set of arguments on which the creed was formulated. Its beginning was written in 1939: its end consists of reprints from *Blast* (1914 and 1915) and *The Tyro* (No. 2) (1924). It is a good book, and it has become a better book with the passage of time. Those concentrated little essays which, when they first appeared in *Blast* thirty-five years ago, seemed largely angry and destructive, now appear surprisingly reasonable and far-seeing—even prophetic. It is not part of my task to analyse them or even to praise them. But it is certain that they would not be half as impressive today if their author had not been a painter. He got rid, in prose, of a good deal of justifiable irritation. He posed his problem in words and then began to find its solution in paint. As an artist he knew just what he wanted: as a writer he knew what he didn't want and didn't like.

When those early essays were written, art was endeavouring to work its way round the awkward curve that separated the nineteenth from the twentieth

17

century. Impressionism was the last phase of the 'truth to appearance' movement that began with the Italian Renaissance. Cubism, Abstract art and Futurism (we have almost forgotten Futurism[1] but in those days it was very vociferous) were throwing 'appearance' overboard and at the same time groping for something to take its place. Today that awkward curve has been rounded—not very gracefully, it is true—and we are showing signs in England of getting into the straight part of the track. Looking back, it becomes clear that Wyndham Lewis was one of the few artists clear-headed enough in 1914 to lead the way to it—certainly the only one capable of formulating the problem in words and solving it in paint.

'Clear-headed' may seem an odd word to use of a creative artist. 'Courageous' or 'imaginative' might seem more appropriate. And at any less transitional moment than the end of the first decade of this century, courage and imagination would have been the right weapons for progress. But when an old mode is obsolescent and a new one overdue, hard thinking as well as strong feeling are necessary. A formula must be found: a 'movement' must be planned: manifestos must be written: an Ism must be born.

During the last hundred years France has been prolific in Isms. It is characteristic of the Frenchman to think before he paints. But in England, when an Ism is born one can be sure that a moment of crisis has arrived. England has only produced two. For one an artist of Italian descent, Rossetti, was responsible: for the other, Wyndham Lewis. Pre-Raphaelitism and Vorticism are both symbolic words, attached to no narrowly definable creed. Nor is it necessary to attempt a definition. What matters is that such labels come into being as a sort of battle-cry. *X est mort: vive Y.* Y must on no account have any X-ness in it.

It is not necessary to explain 'Vorticism' in order to understand Wyndham Lewis. The word itself was coined not by himself but by Ezra Pound in 1913. In the sense that a handful of artists, his contemporaries, shared Lewis's views and were influenced by his mannerisms, Vorticism was a 'movement'. But he was both too individual and too independent to need either a battle-cry or a bodyguard of disciples. He had certain intentions and he carried them out. He is still doing so today. Any artist can explain his intentions since he alone knows them. But no artist can see himself effectively enough to describe the unique quality of what he has done. Exasperating as it may seem to so articulate a person as Wyndham Lewis, he needs an interpreter even though he can be his own historian.

In *Men Without Art, Blasting and Bombardiering* and elsewhere he has been his own historian and also that of his 'period'. And when I speak of his 'period'

[1] Since this essay was written, an exhibition of 'Modern Italian Art' was held at the Tate Gallery under the auspices of the Arts Council in May and June 1950. Some readers will recall the vociferous and turbulent nature of the Futurist exhibits. (ED.)

I do not mean that he is either dead or out of date—he is, to a remarkable extent, neither—but merely that in and after 1912 he sounded the first note of a tune that no one had heard then but with which we are all fairly familiar now. It probably amuses him to hear people in the street whistling it casually without being aware that he was its composer. To speak of Lewis's period is to recognize that he was a prophet. His prophecies have been fulfilled and one tends to forget how long ago he uttered them. Fuseli said of Blake that he was 'damned good to steal from'. There are plenty of young artists in 1950 who steal freely from the Lewis of 1920, and still look furiously up to date. There are a dozen more who use idioms derived from him without knowing whence they came. The eggs he laid have hatched: the clucking with which he announced their arrival is in danger of being forgotten when the newly-hatched chicks begin to cheep.

Mr Lewis's 'period' is the period, in art, of Kandinski and Mondrian and in letters, of T. S. Eliot, James Joyce and Ezra Pound—massive influences, yet I can imagine nothing more depressing to an artist who is now in his prime than to be thought of as an 'influence'. This introduction is concerned neither with Lewis's 'period', which he himself has described in detail, nor with his 'influence', which is widespread and wholesome, but with his paintings and drawings and with the difference between *his* paintings and drawings and those of his predecessors and contemporaries.

The situation, as regards painting and drawing, at the beginning of the 1914–18 war is analysed in considerable detail in *Notes and Vortices II*.[1] Briefly, the argument of the pamphlet is that Impressionism, being concerned with visual truth and nothing else, is no longer serviceable. 'There was a sort of five-mile limit beyond which a Realist must not move. He must paint what is under his nose . . .'. The alternatives are: (1) Cubism, which is only another form of naturalism—equally scientific, equally concerned with what is under the nose—which 'tempts the artist to slip back into facile and sententious formulas and escape invention', (2) Futurism, 'which is always too tyrannically literary . . . too democratic and subjugated by indiscriminate objects', and (3) Abstract art (which he rightly calls 'Expressionism'), which lives outside the 'five-mile limit' in a cul-de-sac of sentiment, dehumanized, unrelated to visual experience of life.

From this impasse how is the artist to emerge? It is at this point that Lewis, shifting his ground from the negative to the positive, begins to reveal his personal passions and prejudices. He is an avowed humanist. Obviously imitating Nature is no good. 'The first reason for not imitating Nature is that you cannot convey the emotion you receive at the contact of Nature by imitating her but only by becoming her.' 'The essence of an object is beyond, and often in contradiction to, its simple, its representational truth.' So far any thinking man would

[1] *Wyndham Lewis the Artist*, p. 131.

agree. But the important question for the individual artist is, 'What, *to me*, is the essence of the object?' For each artist extracts his own 'essence', and each artist, when he 'becomes' Nature, is still himself, and therefore every artist 'becomes' something unlike every other artist, although all of them 'become' Nature. He can only dimly describe that 'essence' in words, and only vaguely tell you what sort of a self he retains when he 'becomes' Nature. Why, after all, should he bother to attempt the description? The 'self' and the 'essence' are both in his picture. That is what his pictures are 'about'. It is the art critic, not the artist, who must try to turn the 'essence of the object' as expressed in the picture, into words. He is a translator, a dealer in second-hand values, which the artist should never be.

Nevertheless, the artist, if he is articulate at all, cannot help hinting at the nature of this essence. Here, for example, is a casual but revealing sentence: 'A rigidity and simplification to a more tense and angular entity (as in the case of Mantegna) has not prejudiced their high place, or the admiration due to several great artists.' That describes, almost by chance, just what Lewis is after, and it links him with the one artist of the past who could share the description with him. Both 'become', when they paint, rigid, tense and angular, though Mantegna, unlike Lewis, doesn't simplify. That, superficially, explains their style. But Lewis goes farther and, in a passage that seems to me one of the profoundest explanations of the creative imagination I have ever read, says, 'Have your breakfast in the ordinary way and, as the result of your hunger and your unconsciousness, on getting up you will find an air of inevitability about the way the various objects . . . lie upon the table, that it would be very difficult to get consciously and deliberately.'

There you have the whole problem and its solution. The impressionist merely records the under-the-nose appearance of the cups and saucers and coffee-pot. The cubist merely treats them as solid objects. The abstract artist turns his back on them and ignores their very existence. The vorticist (I use the word merely as a label for Wyndham Lewis and anyone else who happens to agree with him) sees them as *symbols of hunger and unconsciousness*, and proceeds—somewhere near the edges of the five-mile limit—to give a simple, tense account of them and their inevitability as such. That, surely, is an ambitious but sensible programme.

One more quotation. 'The finest artists—and this is what Art means—are those men who are so trained and sensitized that they have a perpetually renewed power of DOING WHAT NATURE DOES, only doing it with all the beauty of accident, without the certain futility that accident implies.' No artist could better express his intentions. What remains, for the critic, is to decide to what extent the particular artist in question has carried them out in his art. For good intentions are a product of clear-headedness, but good art is a product of imagination and craftsmanship.

Every real artist is capable, in his moments of vision, of 'becoming' Nature. But no artist can ever become more than a small part, or rather a small *aspect* of Nature. The aspect of Nature that Wyndham Lewis becomes could be roughly called the metallic or precise aspect. Whatever in Nature is already precise and clear-cut makes him happy, offers him no problem. It emerges in his drawings magnificently tangible and resistant to the eye. Its shapes are imperturbable and significant. He can play with them as a poet plays with words, charging them with a meaning that far transcends their dictionary meaning. He could, so to speak, draw a locomotive or a howitzer (it is significant that he was an artillery officer in the 1914–18 war) without much conscious effort of 'becoming' metallic or precise. But what of the smoke that emerges from the funnel? What about a tree in the full glory of summer foliage? What about a man? How could a humanist express his humanism by identifying himself with metal? Those are the kind of questions that the art critic usually evades; they compel him to be too specific. But I see no reason for evading them here. Nothing could be more fascinating than to watch Mr Lewis identifying Nature (i.e. his given subject matter) with metal, taking all the really metallic objects in his stride and gently wooing and coaxing the non-metallic objects till they begin to speak with a metallic accent without losing their 'essence'.

Take, for example, a magnificent early painting: 'A Battery Shelled', of 1919 (Pl. 26). Wyndham Lewis won't take the easy way out of making the gun the hero of the picture and turning its context and its attendants into a painted back-cloth. Being a humanist he almost conceals the gun (it is of the first importance in warfare that guns should be concealed). But the mess of crazy, wheel-rutted ground that surrounds it, the dug-out entrances, the bits of corrugated iron, the shattered trees, the members of the gun team, the officers in the foreground—these are really worthy of his close attention. They have to be coaxed and translated until they become the inevitable symbols of scientific violence, disciplined chaos. It would be easy but ineffective to turn them all into metal—metal mackintoshes, metal men. That would be the opposite of humanism. It would also be boring. But they must *hint* at metal: the officers' faces look as though they might have been cast in a mould, even though they are flesh. The members of the gun team are not dressed in armour plating, but neither are they wearing khaki cloth. The rutted earth they stand on is mud, certainly, but carved mud. The rhythm of metal rather than metal itself pervades the picture. A metamorphosis has taken place. Nature has lost, under Lewis's treatment, a great deal of herself. Constable would be horrified at what she has lost. So would Titian. Mantegna would not. But what she has *not* lost has been presented to us as a 'more tense and angular entity' than could ever be found anywhere but in the mind of an unusually creative artist.

It is also surprising to note, as one examines the picture, how much she has not lost. She is as fully three-dimensional and solid as Constable or Titian could desire. One could make one's way step by step from the officers and the blasted tree-trunks in the foreground across the intermediate carved-mud wilderness peopled with active automata, to the gun, and beyond it to the three shell-bursts in the distance; one could equally travel into the picture through the air, following the formalized banner of drifting smoke.

It is by no means his best painting, though it is as complete a factual account of one aspect of modern war as I have seen. But it provides a key to his style. One can work backwards from it to the pre-war drawings of which the 'Centauress' (1912) and the crowded drawing from the 'Timon of Athens' series (1913) are examples. Or one can work forward to the more flexible and more skilful drawings done between the wars. The 'Timon' drawing (Pl. 3) is a very remarkable achievement; it presents one with a convincing world, a world made of nothing but harsh angles and arcs of circles, an ordered pandemonium of a world in which, one would have thought, nothing organic could live. Yet not only do Alcibiades and two of his lady friends, and groups of soldiers in the distance and middle distance, manage to live in it: they are an integral part of it: they have characters of their own and they perform their parts in the drama.

That is a difficult creative act to have accomplished. It is precisely the poet's act, the counterpart of the feat whereby a writer takes the world of words and, extracting from it those that will serve his purpose, drills and regiments them, imposes rhythms on them, marshals them into little squads full of verbal energy, yet never robs them of their meaning—gives them, in fact, not a new but an intensified meaning. The 'Timon' drawing was done, of course, at a moment when art had become unusually conscious of the possibilities of this kind of regimenting. Pound, Eliot and Joyce were juggling with words in much the same way that Lewis was juggling with shapes. Joyce, in the end, juggled so skilfully that they became uncomfortably charged with meaning. In the second decade of this century both words and shapes became more potent instruments. The tools at the disposal of the artist and the writer became more precise and more expressive. As it turned out, most artists were incapable of using them to advantage since they had little to express. But the credit for the fashioning of those artists' tools is largely due to Wyndham Lewis.

The 'Timon' drawing shows these tools in the making, used with virtuosity but with less skill than later drawings. The 'Girl in a Windsor Chair' of 1920 (Pl. 28) is drawn with the precision of a lathe. Direction, pressure on the pencil point, the relation of curve to curve, curve to straight, are all under control. The girl and the chair have become as beautiful (I use the word in its strictest sense) as a violin and much more complex. A sheaf of violins, seen from every angle, and thought of not only as a linear arabesque but also sculpturally, would be a closer analogy. Such precision of control could only arrive after years of hard slogging. Mantegna would have done the same thing with equal precision, and with far more affection but with less freedom, less power to turn a pencil line into a whiplash, and less positive delight in manipulating the whip. After Mantegna, who?

The word 'whiplash' reminds me that neither skill nor a love of the cool and the metallic (with which, of course, goes a positive hatred of softness and warmth: Wyndham Lewis and Matthew Smith are *exact* opposites) are enough to explain the emotional undertones of an artist's work. 'Whiplash' suggests castigation; the whip, elegantly used, is the satirist's weapon. It is here, on this deeper level, that Mantegna and Wyndham Lewis cease to have anything in common. Mantegna is no satirist. In Wyndham Lewis's work there is always an undercurrent of satire. His subject-matter may be as innocent as a daisy but the resultant work of art suggests a cynical frame of mind, a refusal to be taken in by false sentiment and a consequent mistrust of *any* sentiment. His imaginative paintings are never of a desirable world, his sitters are rarely heroes and heroines. In 1932 he published *Thirty Personalities and a Self-Portrait*—a portfolio of reproductions from pencil drawings. Since he is an exceptionally good draughtsman they are all good as drawings: being interested in people, he has brought them all to life: being keenly observant, he has produced likenesses without resorting to caricature. But, having a satirical mind, he has expressed an opinion about each of his sitters. They are comments—by no means all unfavourable—as well as likenesses. And that capacity to comment—that incapacity not to comment—is an invariable characteristic of his work. Most of the 'Thirty Personalities' are seen critically and intellectually, but in two of them a hint of heroine-worship may be detected. There is something of the Greek Goddess in his Naomi Mitchison and Rebecca West is seen as a novelist sees the heroine he has created.

Even in a brief essay on the work of an artist, and even though Mr Handley-Read's Chronological Outline in this book will supply the reader with the kind of detail that would be out of place here, one or two biographical references are not irrelevant. Wyndham Lewis was born in December 1884. The birthdays of his literary contemporaries are, in the words of one of them, 'scattered up and down the eighties'. Eighteen rather useless months at the Slade followed by a migration—an inevitable migration—to Paris, a short trip to Spain, another to Munich, another to Holland, form a restless prelude to a return to England about 1910. It was a necessary but not a creative prelude. Doubtless a lot of drawings and paintings were done, but few of them survive and those that do reveal a man who was too busy absorbing to think much about producing. One thing is noteworthy. His friends in Paris were Spanish Americans: he learned Spanish: he visited Spain. Italy was no magnet. Lewis would certainly wish to be called a classic artist rather than a romantic one (he has often attempted to define the distinction), yet he avoided the Mediterranean source of classicism and preferred the hard cold realism of Spain to the poetized idealism of Italy. The truth is, of course, that the popular opposition of romantic to classic is a false one and that Lewis, despite his own theories about himself, is a romantic, but a hard instead of a mushy one. The spiky silhouettes, the twisting vertical rhythms he creates are nearer to a Gothic cathedral than to a Greek temple. The full implications of this must be discussed later. The predilection for Spain is here recorded as evidence of his temperament, not in order to furnish him with a label.

An important incident is the purchase of a picture in 1911 by Augustus John. The picture seems to have disappeared. It was called 'The Yellow Fishermen' and it was evidently not an abstract design.

Illnesses, the appearance of *Blast* (sure first sign of the militant Irrepressible), a stormy connection with Roger Fry and the Omega workshops, a defiant exit therefrom and the setting up of the Rebel Art Centre in 1914, the second or 'War' number of *Blast* (equally provocative), the war itself and service as an officer in the Siege Artillery, the peace, the publication (1918) of the first novel, *Tarr*, and the first one-man show at the Goupil Galleries in February 1919, were the chief events of what might be called Lewis's 'formative' period. It was a period in which a good deal of heart-searching occurred and a good many problems were solved.

Those problems seem to have lost much of their importance now. One is a little puzzled by the seriousness with which the question of 'abstract' versus 'realistic' or 'figurative' art was argued. Today the battle, on which at that time so much seemed to depend, has been neither lost nor won. In retrospect it can be seen as no battle at all but merely a decision which every artist can make for himself according to what he has to say. Lewis has produced both abstract art (especially in 1912–15) and also whatever is the term for non-abstract art. He has even thought it necessary to be defiant or apologetic or explanatory about which of the two is 'right'. I can no more join in that controversy today, vital though the issue may have been thirty years ago, than I can think it important to define 'Vorticism' or to decide whether Lewis is a romantic or a classic. To me the issue seems simple and labels of this kind merely confuse it. The issue is surely this. An artist is a man who does two things. He absorbs experience, mostly through his eye, but also by every other means at his disposal as a human being. (He can absorb it, for example, by reading Shakespeare's *Timon of Athens*.) He then recreates that experience by inventing shapes, colours, rhythms, juxtapositions, and by transferring his inventions to paper or canvas. Whether he has experienced pure spikiness (perhaps by remembering a thistle, or perhaps by looking at Mr So-and-so's profile) or whether he has experienced a dream about wandering along a rocky shore, or whether he has gazed hard at Mr So-and-so's full face as a preliminary to painting his portrait, it is not necessary that he should justify himself in the eyes of the world by announcing that his intentions are abstract or unabstract. He is a creator, an inventor of shapes and juxtapositions. He can invent spikes that are no more than good or bad spikes, or he can invent spikes that describe something that he saw when he looked at Mr So-and-so, and which therefore turn out to be a stylized portrait of that personage. This too can be good or bad. He is, in fact, judged by his power to recreate vividly his experience and to please us by doing so. Whether his shapes are called a 'portrait' or a 'dream picture' or a 'design', whether they are Vorticist or Cubist, Classic or Romantic, is surely unimportant. The labels are names for categories, and if an artist breathes more easily in category A than in category B let him take up his stand there. He does no more than explain his own point of view when he attempts to arrange the categories in order of merit or explains why he has deserted A and will be henceforth loyal to B.

But it is of immense importance that his shapes—whether they are called 'design' or 'dream' or 'portrait'—should be expressive, eloquent shapes. If he cannot invent a visual equivalent for his experience he is a failure.

Once that is granted the rest of this essay can deal with one question only. It can be called 'Wyndham Lewis, Inventor and Creator', and the only question worth discussing is: 'Given his personal set of predilections which, as already mentioned, are rather like those of Mantegna, has Mr Lewis succeeded in finding the right shapes for Timon or T. S. Eliot or the "Surrender of Barcelona"?'

In my opinion he is one of the great inventors. The muscular urge—some trick of the wrist or of the fingers—that guides his pen or pencil is as recognizable as that of any artist known to me. That whiplash quality, already referred to, or the queer curves set up when a breaking wave meets the backwash of its predecessor, or the lines of a salmon's back and dorsal fin when it leaps a waterfall— those are the kind of curves that form his vocabulary. But to ascribe them to a muscular urge is to trace them only halfway to their home. The muscles obey the brain, and though only intuition can trace the connection between the arabesque of a whiplash and the state of mind of the man who wields the whip, the connection is evident. To anyone trained in the 'reading' of a work of art there is not much difficulty in guessing at the courage, the intelligence, the love of precision, the hatred of mystery, the insatiable visual curiosity in anything that moves or grows, the boredom with anything static or indolent, that dictate those muscular twinges in the fingers holding the brush or pencil. A glance at almost any plate in the book will confirm such a guess, but if the reader wishes me to be specific let him look at the drawing on the cover of *The Enemy* (No. 1) for January 1927.

The effect of that half-abstract mounted Japanese warrior, part totem pole, part beetle, part man, made up of overlapping or interlocking plates, with jewel-like eyes at the joints, is certainly inimical. The shape of the whole is so solid and impenetrable, yet little ragged points break the smooth surface everywhere—the horse's mane, the saddle, the impossibly pointed forelegs (hooves would have given the effect of a false quantity or a broken rhyme sequence)—and turn the spectator's eye into a pincushion. If this is not a *Gothic* drawing (Spanish Gothic, perhaps), despite the Japanese accent of it, I have misunderstood the meaning of Gothic. Yet a Gothic cathedral is, I suppose, an example of pure abstract art, and this is certainly not. There is as much horse-ness in this horse as in any of the justly praised horses drawn by palaeolithic man or George Stubbs.

But this drawing belongs to a later period—one can call it the 'mature' period if one wishes to tabulate—when Lewis had presumably ceased to worry about the justification of 'abstract' or 'near-abstract'. That period began in about 1920. Drawings of all kinds, some pure drawings of 'observation', others inventive, and a good many portraits were shown in his second exhibition (called 'Tyros and Portraits') at the Leicester Galleries in April 1921. More paintings, drawings, more portraits followed, until their place began to be taken, between the years 1926 and 1932, by a succession of books surprising enough in a career entirely devoted to literature but hardly credible for a man who still continued to draw and paint, though less prolifically than during the preceding years.

As the spate of books eased off a new note crept into the paintings—a more literary, perhaps a more surrealist note. What happened, in simple language, was that Wyndham Lewis began to create a kind of private mythology which envisaged a world mysteriously peopled by robots of various kinds, living a remote life of their own, based, as always happens in imaginative art, on the subconscious processes of the artist. The reader must forgive the introduction of the bedraggled and misused word 'subconscious'. Our terminology for the ways of the human mind is at present hopelessly inadequate. The vague word 'subconscious' must do duty for something more precise which I will attempt to define in the next paragraph.

Obviously pictures like this require a more or less literary interpretation. 'What does it mean?' is the normal man's question before a painting that seems to suggest a mixture of mysticism and satire. Yet a *close* or detailed literary interpretation is always impossible. Chirico's more obviously romantic and metaphysical early paintings, though utterly different in style and content, tackle the same level of experience and demand the same approach. It is easy to say that in such paintings an artist draws on a set of unconscious impulses or that some illogical subconscious dictator whispers in his ear as he paints and that he listens more attentively than he would if he were painting a portrait. That is a half-truth, but when one remembers that Giorgione's 'Tempestà' and Dürer's 'Knight and Death', to mention two out of ten million works of art, were the result of listening to the same whisper, it is evidently an insufficient answer to the normal man's 'What does it mean?' All artists sink an artesian well into their own subconscious minds when they begin to paint, but all imaginative paintings do not puzzle the normal man by their content. Confronted by

Giorgione he says 'How delightful!', by Hieronymus Bosch 'How queer!', never 'What does it mean?' Wyndham Lewis is different. There is in these explorations done in the late thirties something private and elusive. Giorgione and Dürer and Hieronymus Bosch bring back strange specimens from their travels, but they are recognizably of this world, like orchids and prickly pears and flying fish. Wyndham Lewis's specimens are either from a dream world or from the moon. The familiar vocabulary is there, but the syntax, the shape of the sentences is unfamiliar, and unless the spectator is prepared to accept that unfamiliarity and let it work its *visual* will on him instead of closing his eyes and asking questions about the literary content, he will not respond. Or, rather, he will only respond to the vocabulary.

I am willing to admit that this is a disadvantage, but there is no escape from it. If a man returns from the moon with a set of specimens that cannot be classified as known genera or species he asks a good deal of his public—at first. For the public, it appears, can tolerate abstract and near-abstract art up to a point. It knows that 'form' is an essential part of art, and when it finds a great deal of form and very little appreciable content in a painting it sighs regretfully that there should be so much to look at and so little to think about; but it does at least look. But when the painting seems to be full of content, and yet that content is baffling to the normal processes of thought, how is the artist to persuade his public that it will be worth their while to practise a slightly abnormal process of thought in order to settle down comfortably in the world he has created and to recognize its inhabitants as brothers and sisters? How is he to get his specimens accepted? He can only go on producing more and more specimens until there are enough of them to be classified by comparing one with another. Great artists have always done this until a moment arrived when they had created enough to furnish a classifiable world with its own fauna and flora. It is then the task of the spectator, aided by the critic, to attempt his own classification. And this is precisely what Mr Handley-Read, in his essay, has done.

I am not sure that Lewis has created quite enough. Those little ball-headed creatures that inhabit the 'Mud Clinic' (Pl. 21) become more convincing when they reappear in 'Tank in the Clinic'. We know more about them, and we want to know more still. They evidently live a highly organized life and think a great deal about the care of their bodies. We come across them again but in a different mood in 'Stations of the Dead' (Pl. 19), hanging about in groups, waiting for something, in the shadow of something at entrances that lead to something. And here they are again, more stylishly dressed and in a more lavish part of the moon, in 'Four Figure Composition' (Pl. 23). (The lavishness depends on nothing more than the presence of a great many circular objects and fluent curves, so closely are form and content interdependent.) And three of them—little minxes, escaped from the moon for a weekend on the South Coast—have been spotted by Mr Lewis and compelled to sit for their portraits in 'Beach Babies (Pl. 13).

In the 'Surrender of Barcelona' (1936) (Pl. 16) Wyndham Lewis was only half-way to the moon. Or if he had arrived he was still feeling a little nostalgic about the earth. Memories of Velasquez's spears from the 'Surrender of Breda', memories of Cortez, of New York, of petrol tanks, cling about him, narrowing the through route to his subconscious mind and making the picture more 'intelligible' from a literary point of view. But it is worth while, in parenthesis, to insist that the question 'What does it mean?' though natural, is unreasonable. What does the room in which I am writing 'mean'? What do the cups and saucers and coffee-pot left on the table after breakfast 'mean'? Wyndham Lewis has given his answer. To him they are inevitably arranged symbols of hunger. That is how his mind works. To Monet they were coloured objects catching the light. To Cézanne they were interesting specimens of structure.

But from these excursions to the moon Wyndham Lewis returned with an eye more sensitive to terrestrial possibilities. Compare the drawing 'Woman in an Armchair' of 1936 (Pl. 38) with the drawing 'Girl in a Windsor Chair' of 1920 (Pl. 28) already mentioned. Both are factual drawings from a seated model and both use the same oddly vital shapes that are Wyndham Lewis's own invention—his signature tune—but the later drawing 'means' more. One can explain that either by saying that it is more human or (and I suspect that this comes to the same thing) that the artesian well to the unconscious mind has, in the intervening years, been driven deeper.

It was this added depth that made the fourth one-man show, held at the Leicester Galleries in December 1937, the most important up to that date. The full range of his work as a draughtsman, as a portrait painter and as an imaginative explorer was now visible. And the connection between the three aspects of him could be seen. Why, between the exhibition and the outbreak of war two years later, he abandoned the moon and produced mainly portrait drawings and portraits in oils, I cannot tell. The answer may have something to do with economics, or it may be that an alternating rhythm between imagination and fact is necessary for a balanced life. Portraiture has occupied more than half of Lewis's working life. Up to the present moment his output of paintings has been divided, in about the same proportion as Goya's, between 'subject pictures' and portraiture. He is, in fact, the best kind of portrait painter because he is not, like Franz Hals or Romney, a professional portrait painter. The isolated human being is for him merely a specialized kind of 'subject'.

Portraiture is at present under a cloud. A suspicion has established itself that there is something artistically degrading about the practice of it, that the obligation to produce a likeness carries with it a stigma from which there is no escaping. It is true that the ability to produce a likeness is often accompanied by a strange lack of ability to do anything else, except perhaps to apply paint to canvas in a breezy or a sentimental or a painstaking way. The reverse proposition—that a creative artist, even if he has the gift to produce a likeness, is wasting his precious time and his poetic soul if he attempts it—is fashionable but untrue.

The question can be settled not by solemnly arguing the case for portraiture as a truly creative branch of painting but by looking at the series of portraits by Wyndham Lewis, beginning with the self-portrait of 1921 and brought up to date by T. S. Eliot of 1949 (Pl. B). Everything that has already been said about distilling the 'essence of the object' and 'becoming Nature' is as applicable to a picture of Miss Sitwell in her environment as to one of a group of moon-denizens in theirs. There is a slight change of emphasis. Miss Sitwell tends to dominate her environment: the moon-denizens are absorbed by theirs. Also the painter meets her face to face in the same room whereas he has to spy on his moon-people through the keyhole. They are unaware that their lives are exposed to view.

But, granted this difference between the artist as visible friend and the artist as invisible spy, the problem for both is the same and the development is the same. The problem is to seize on the particular essence of a given human being which the artist is, at the moment of painting, capable of extracting. The development, from the early 'twenties to the late 'thirties, is a steady humanizing process. By that I do not mean that the sitters become less precise and more fleshy, but that they become more capable of doing the things that make human beings interesting. The 'Self-Portrait' of 1923 can hardly be thought of as being ready to smile or grumble or light a cigarette. The Ezra Pound of 1938 will certainly do all these things as soon as he opens his eyes.

But within the limits of this humanizing process, all the portraits have the familiar 'tense and angular entity' that one would expect. They are individualized (which is not the same as 'humanized') to a surprising degree. One would, of course, expect them to have fully recognizable eyes and noses and mouths, for Lewis is a superb draughtsman, but individualism goes much farther than that. It permeates the whole canvas. His sitter's hands (hands are an obsession with him), the texture of his skin, the coarseness or fineness of his hair, his very clothes are registered with extreme exactness. Stephen Spender's nose, hair, fingers, shirt-collar, have a pervading, large unruliness. John MacLeod has a rococo elegance, Naomi Mitchison a compact softness, T. S. Eliot (the 1938 version) a hieratic deliberateness.[1]

For an artist who has already been described as having a natural sympathy for the precise and the structural, this is extraordinary. For human beings are not made of metal, and though nothing is easier for an artist than to subject them to the kind of metamorphosis that will cause them to reappear on the canvas as so many robots, nothing could be more difficult than to paint a series of robots who still retain all the little oddnesses, quickness, slowness, softness, hardness, ruthlessness, gentleness, that differentiate one human being from

[1] The four portraits mentioned are reproduced on Pls. 42, 48, 43 and 40 respectively.

another. Even these simple and generalized characteristics belong to types rather than to persons. Yet Wyndham Lewis's portraits are, to a greater extent than those of any painter but Goya, descriptions of persons. But whereas Goya achieved his effect of revealing personality by giving his sitters the kind of animation that results when artist and sitter are conversing or quarrelling, Lewis's portraits seem to be the result of a penetrating silent observation. The sitter emerges as a *shape*—always a Gothic shape, but 'Gothic' can be as various in its manifestations as can 'human'. I have already noted how the fluent and circular shapes in 'Four Figure Composition' (Pl. 23) set the mood of the picture, since form and content are merely names for the obverse and reverse of the same medal. Even so—even more so—does Wyndham Lewis in his portraits discover the shapes appropriate to the character of the sitter. They bulge, they produce crockets and finials and buttresses with admirable inevitability. That is what makes them 'good' portraits as well as good pictures. The 1938 Eliot (Pl. 40), for instance, is shaped very roughly like a crossbow. Any artist can decide to use a composition based on a crossbow: to do so requires a minimum of imagination. But to produce a crossbow made of curves that could only come from the Lewis visual vocabulary and yet convince the spectator that Eliot is more Eliotish *because* he is shaped like a crossbow—that is beyond the power of critical analysis. It is the kind of process by which only the best portraits are painted.

No more need be said about the portraits. They speak for themselves, and the normal man, who feels quite at home in the presence of human beings, is never tempted to ask 'What do they mean?' Perhaps I have already wasted too many words on what I think they mean. In one sense they are among Lewis's most satisfying works, since they are inevitably simpler in shape, bigger in the design of their main masses, than his dream pictures. And because their pattern is bigger (and *not* because their content is easier) they hit harder. One or two—the best of them—are situated not far from the edge of the dream world. Indeed, the 'Red Portrait' of 1937 (Pl. 41) is actually on the frontier. It is either an unusually haunting portrait or an unusually reassuring dream, according to which side of the frontier it is seen from.

Throughout this essay I have considered Wyndham Lewis primarily as a creator in terms of form rather than a colourist. Therein lies his chief importance as an originator, and in that he is typically British. The fierce vitality of his black and white drawings, the urgency of movement implicit in their curves and angles, need no help from colour. And the icy precision of his pencil in the drawings of the 'twenties would be weakened by anything but the palest colour washes. But no large-scale painter can afford to neglect colour and no artist who, like Wyndham Lewis, wishes 'to convey the emotion received at the contact with Nature', can regard colour as anything but an additional and an important means of conveying emotion.

Here a difficulty arises which few born draughtsmen have ever succeeded in overcoming. To use colour emotionally without thereby interfering with the impact of the form is almost impossible. Van Gogh, an adequate draughtsman but not an inventive one, who was certainly a creator of rhythm but hardly ever of form, could make his colour bear the major part of the picture's burden. His tell-tale rhythms could find expression as easily in the brush-stroke as in the pen-stroke. Gauguin, a clumsy draughtsman, was lost without colour. But the most that Wyndham Lewis, whose emotional meaning is already expressed in his drawing, can hope for is that his colour will reinforce that emotional meaning, and the least is that it will not contradict it. The full delectable orchestration of colour of a decorator like Matisse is denied him. He is presumably content that it should be so. He comes near to *decorative* or heraldic colour in the early self-portrait. But the undeniably *expressive* colour of his imaginative paintings is almost as personal as his form. It, too, is metallic. Steely greys and steely blues perform contrapuntally against the pervasive dull reds of red-hot steel or the browns and yellows of rusted iron or the warmer tang of polished copper. Occasionally, where a note of pageantry in the picture itself demands it —in the 'Surrender of Barcelona' (Pl. 16), for instance—a gayer heraldic note creeps in, but the sensuous orchestra without which a Matisse or a Matthew Smith would be nothing is useless to him. He can extract all the colour he needs from a string quartette. His colour is astringent, unexpected and as personal as his form. It is not a mere addition to his form. It came into being, in his mind's eye, simultaneously with the form and is the exact counterpart of it, just as a melody carries with it, in the mind's ear the precise harmonies without which it cannot achieve its full poignancy.

It is not by accident that, in the last analysis, one describes the visual arts in musical terms. Once subject-matter has been left behind, nothing remains but harmony of colour, melody of line and timbre of paint. Wyndham Lewis is temperamentally related to Bach. It is a rough-and-ready description, but it does account for the austerity, the intelligence, the crispness and the coldness. Yet through the coldness of the formal construction, just as with Bach, there often breaks an oddly haunting, romantic song.

2

Chronological Outline

C. THE CONVALESCENT

Chronological Outline

Besides giving facts of biography, and a record of exhibitions, these notes are intended to indicate the *kind* of work produced stage by stage throughout Wyndham Lewis's career up to the present. For this purpose, outstanding examples from each year have been quoted, with special reference to paintings and drawings in public galleries and museums. Also, because his work as an artist and as an author has sometimes been closely related, and as he is unique at the present time in being articulate, and to the same extent productive in both capacities, a hand-list is included of his very numerous publications.[1] This list does not include all the pamphlets.

The following abbreviations have been used extensively throughout the Chronological Outline; in the footnotes to the essay 'Detail in the Style of Wyndham Lewis'; and throughout the Notes on the Plates:

Baker Collection, V&AM.: A group of 27 examples of Wyndham Lewis's work in the possession of the Victoria and Albert Museum, South Kensington. With some gaps this collection represents the artist between 1909 and 1917. The following note is printed beneath each drawing:
'Presented by the Family of the late Capt Guy Baker in accordance with his expressed wishes.' Guy Baker was a friend of the artist who died at the end of the 1914–18 war.

Carlow Collection: Assembled by the late Lord Carlow, the collection includes numerous original holograph manuscripts of Wyndham Lewis's books, together with many corrected galley- and page-proofs; a number of original drawings signed by the artist, of which several are unpublished; and a large collection of miscellaneous matter related to his work as an artist and writer—material connected with the periodicals, advertisements, press cuttings; also exhibition invitation cards, etc. Much of the manuscript material was specially bound by Lord Carlow. The collection also includes seventeen first editions of the literary publications, all signed and inscribed by the author. Present owner: A. Zwemmer, Esq.

R.G.R.E.: The Redfern Gallery Retrospective Exhibition of Wyndham Lewis's paintings and drawings, May 1949. (See further notes on this exhibition, p. 47.)

Rutherston Collection: The Rutherston Loan Scheme, City Art Gallery, Manchester. With several gaps, the twenty-four drawings by Wyndham Lewis in this collection include

---

[1] For a full bibliography of Wyndham Lewis's works up to the end of 1931 (including details of collation), the reader is referred to *Apes, Japes and Hitlerism* by John Gawsworth, Unicorn Press (first published 1932). With the exception of the three publications of 1940, 1941 and 1942 (see p. 47), the details given in my 'hand-list' have all been checked by reference to actual copies of the books, folios or journals. As far as they go these details accord substantially with those of Mr Gawsworth (whose list ends with the *Diabolical Principle* of 1931).

examples of the artist's work as a draughtsman between the years 1911 and 1921. There is one painting in oils: the SELF PORTRAIT OF THE ARTIST (Frontispiece). The beginning of the Loan Scheme, which now (1950) includes about 1,600 pictures by twentieth-century artists, dates from 1925, when the late Charles Rutherston presented the Gallery with some 800 modern pictures on condition that they were to be available for loan to schools, colleges of art, and other educational institutions in the North of England.

Lastly, while the question of abbreviation does not arise, it nevertheless seems fitting to record here the pictures by Wyndham Lewis in the National Collection:

The Tate Gallery, Millbank: Four examples of Wyndham Lewis's work are entered in the Catalogue (1947) of the British School: RED SCENE (4913); PORTRAIT OF EDITH SITWELL (5437) (Pl. 37); LA SUERTE (5039); PORTRAIT OF EZRA POUND (5042) (Pl. 47). Since the 1947 catalogue was compiled the gallery has acquired the SURRENDER OF BARCELONA (5768) (Pl. 16), thus making a total of five oil paintings. During 1949 a drawing in colour was exhibited among 'Recent Acquisitions' under the title FRONTISPIECE TO TIMON OF ATHENS[1] (5886). The oil paintings are all mentioned under the appropriate years, below.

1884   Wyndham Lewis born in Nova Scotia.

1897–8 Two years at Rugby School.

1899–1901   A student at the Slade School of Art.

1902   The earliest surviving signed and dated drawing, a life-study preserved with two similar examples at the Slade. Probably made before the artist left England.

1902–8 Extensive visits to France, Germany, Holland and Spain, very important to the artist's early training. In Paris, a studio in the Rue Delambre, in Munich, six months at the Heimann Academy. No examples of much experimental work done abroad can be traced, probably none survive.

1909   Return to England. The artist's style emerges. Studies of heads and figures, sometimes satirical, with fine ink washes of bright blue and yellow as in the THEATRE MANAGER, Baker Collection, V&AM. Work occasionally exhibited at the Ryder Gallery.

1910   Experimental work, few examples survive. The BABY'S HEAD, Baker Collection, V&AM, is one of the very few drawings of children in Wyndham Lewis's work.

1911   First drawings of rock-like figures, as in the GIRL ASLEEP, Rutherston Collection. A member of the newly-formed Camden Town Group under the Presidency of Spencer Gore.

1912   Gouache drawings of rock-like, archaic figures against moon-landscapes, as in TWO FIGURES (Pl. 1, note p. 83); numerous drawings in pen, ink and wash of figures in violent movement; also the first drawings, now recognized as Vorticist, with plan-like backgrounds as in CENTAURESS (Pl. 5, note p. 85). Vorticism not well known until 1914. Over twenty drawings from this year form the first large surviving body of work.

[1] This example, dated 1913, resembles the 'plan' drawings of that year, but it is not reproduced in the publication *Timon of Athens*. (See the notes for 1913 and the entry under *Publications*, 1914.)

1913   Numerous Vorticist drawings. The style typified by totally abstract, flat and plan-like examples, e.g. PLANNERS (Pl. 4, note p. 85); and by the TIMON series represented in *Timon of Athens*: see design from the publication (Pl. 3, note p. 84). Other examples combine box-like figures with angular backgrounds, as in CACTUS,[1] Baker Collection, V&AM. The term 'Vorticist' first used by Ezra Pound.

     The following decorations in oil, important in this year's work, have all been destroyed: an overmantel in the house of Lady Drogheda (reproduced in *Blast*, No. 1, vii); murals in the house of Miss Violet Hunt (Mrs Ford Madox Ford); decorations for Mrs Strindberg at the 'Cave of the Golden Calf'; and murals for the Eiffel Tower restaurant, lately of Percy Street.

1914   Further Vorticist drawings. The movement launched before the public, its chief vehicle being *Blast*. The Rebel Art Centre founded with offices in Great Ormond Street. The first novel, *Tarr*, written during an illness towards the end of the year, not published in book form until 1918.

     The first portrait of Ezra Pound completed this year, a long upright canvas, one of the earliest recorded portraits in oil. Exhibited at the Goupil Gallery, last seen on removal from the exhibition. Untraceable.

PUBLICATIONS

Timon of Athens, the Cube Press. Undated. A folio containing twenty drawings on sixteen unnumbered sheets: six in colour, the remainder in black and white. Originally sent out in an envelope bearing the design (not reproduced within) used on the folio cover. Wyndham Lewis's first publication.

     Blast: Review of the Great English Vortex, No. 1, edited by Wyndham Lewis. John Lane, the Bodley Head. In a puce cover with reproductions of work by Gaudier-Brzeska, Jacob Epstein, Frederick Etchells, Spencer Gore, Cuthbert Hamilton, William Roberts and Wyndham Lewis (six examples). Including the first version of the play *The Enemy of the Stars*.

1915   Further Vorticist drawings. On recovering from his illness, Wyndham Lewis joined the Army. Vorticism henceforth abandoned though characteristics of the style remained. Abstract drawings do not reappear until 1921, then in an entirely different form.

EXHIBITION

In June, at the Doré Gallery, then in New Bond Street, the 'First' Vorticist Exhibition. (No other exhibitions were held under this title.) Organized by Wyndham Lewis, the artist also wrote an introduction

[1] Reproduced in *Twentieth Century Drawings* by Graham Reynolds, Pleiades Books (first published 1946), Pl. 31.

for the catalogue explaining the work and the aims of the movement. The Vorticist Group included Jessie Dismorr, Frederick Etchells, Gaudier-Brzeska, William Roberts, Sanders, Edward Wadsworth and Wyndham Lewis. Of the artist's four pictures then exhibited RED DUET was reproduced in the catalogue, also in *Blast*, No. 2, p. 63. Wyndham Lewis also contributed six woodcuts. Six other artists, not then all Vorticists, were invited to exhibit at the same time: Adeney, Atkinson, Bomberg, Duncan Grant, Kramer and C. R. W. Nevinson, the last noted in the catalogue as a Futurist. Eight examples of sculpture were exhibited by Gaudier-Brzeska, three being lent by Ezra Pound.

A copy of the poster for this exhibition is in the Carlow Collection.

PUBLICATION

Blast: Review of the Great English Vortex, No. 2, edited by Wyndham Lewis. John Lane, the Bodley Head. In a white paper cover designed and lettered by the artist, with reproduction of work by Jessie Dismorr, Frederick Etchells, Gaudier-Brzeska, Jacob Kramer, C. R. W. Nevinson, William Roberts, Sanders, Shakespeare, Edward Wadsworth and Wyndham Lewis (two examples).

1916 Spent in army training, the latter half of the year in France. No examples can be traced.

PUBLICATION

Suitably edited by the author for complete serial publication, the first long instalment of the novel *Tarr* appeared in the April number of *The Egoist*, where it ran without interruption until November 1917. (No issue, March 1917.) The Editors of *The Egoist* then were Richard Aldington, T. S. Eliot and Miss Harriet Weaver.

1917 Seconded as a war artist to the Canadian Corps Headquarters at Vimy Ridge (with the naval guns and a howitzer battery). Numerous drawings of the battery in pen, pencil, chalk and wash. Also less formal drawings of life in France during the war, including MARKET WOMEN: SATURDAY: DIEPPE and other examples in the Baker Collection, V&AM. Several examples from this and the following year were included in the exhibition of 1919.

PUBLICATION

The Ideal Giant: The Code of a Herdsman: Cantelman's Spring Mate: Shield and Spring. Privately printed for *The Little Review*. A pamphlet corded between cardboard covers. With a design on the half-title page also reproduced on the front cover. Proofs, etc., in the Carlow collection.

1918 Numerous war drawings, including a BATTERY POSITION IN A WOOD, Imperial War Museum, London: and a drawing and a large oil-painting

38

both with the title A CANADIAN GUNPIT in the National Gallery of Canada, Ottawa.

PUBLICATION

Tarr, the Egoist Press. Also published a few weeks previously[1] by Alfred A. Knopf, New York. Typescripts and galley-proofs, corrected in the author's hand, with new material in autograph manuscript (published in the edition of 1928), are in the Carlow Collection.

1919   After a very severe illness with 'trench fever' at Etaples, Wyndham Lewis returned to his own Battery on the French coast, then went home on leave. Demobilization followed about a year after the Armistice. After the exhibition, numerous life and portrait drawings, including RED NUDE (Pl. 27, note p. 93), now in the British Council collection; and GIRL LOOKING DOWN, a pencil drawing of Mary Webb (Pl. 29, note p. 93). In the life drawings, a frequent use of strong washes, red-brown, blue, green. Also produced after the exhibition was the very large war scene A BATTERY SHELLED (Pl. 26, note p. 92), in the Imperial War Museum, London.

EXHIBITION

In February, at the Goupil Gallery, the first exhibition 'Guns', paintings and drawings of the war. In the catalogue a Foreword by the artist, and notes on many of the pictures, explaining details of style and choice of subject in the fifty-four exhibits; a 'series dealing with the gunner's life from his arrival in the depot to his life in the line'.

PUBLICATIONS

The Caliph's Design: Architects! where is Your Vortex? The Egoist Press. Corrected galley-proofs, together with an annotated first edition (forming the text for the revised version included in *Wyndham Lewis the Artist: from Blast to Burlington House*, 1939), are in the Carlow Collection.

Wyndham Lewis: Fifteen Drawings, the Ovid Press. With a written certificate of limitation (250 copies), signed or initialled by John Rodker. A folio of fifteen drawings including the well-known POLE JUMP.[2] The drawing GROUP reproduced on the folio cover.

Harold Gilman: An Appreciation, Chatto and Windus. Essays by Wyndham Lewis and Louis F. Ferguson. With thirty-six reproductions of Gilman's work, one in colour.

1920   Work in preparation for the exhibition of the following year. Life drawings show frequent use of sharp *conté* crayon, as in GIRL SEATED

[1] For this detail I am indebted to Gawsworth, *op. cit.*

[2] Reproduced in *English Painting* by R. H. Wilenski, Faber and Faber (first published 1933). Pl. 90.

IN A WINDSOR CHAIR (Pl. 28, note p. 93), one of ten examples of this year's work in the Rutherston Collection.

1921   Further work in preparation for the exhibition. Portraits in oil include PRAXITELLA, Temple Newsam House, Leeds, and PORTRAIT OF THE ARTIST (frontispiece, note p. 81), Rutherston Collection. Among the portrait drawings in *conté* crayon, at least six of Ezra Pound. Later in the year, after the exhibition, the first non-Vorticist abstract drawings.

EXHIBITION

In April, the second exhibition 'Tyros and Portraits', the first of two exhibitions at the Leicester Galleries. A Foreword in the catalogue by the artist with a note on 'Tyros'. Forty-four exhibits, all portraits or figure studies, with a majority of drawings, many washed in colour.

1922   The beginning of a period of semi-retirement lasting nearly four years. Wyndham Lewis then living at the Adam and Eve Mews. It was partly due to incessant hard work at this time that the artist acquired his very great skill as a draughtsman. Much work destroyed. A holiday in Venice in October recorded by various drawings, including one of buildings (see p. 69). In this year the first use, unsupported by other colours, of the well-known pale yellow wash in life and portrait drawings—a characteristic of many later examples.

1923   Semi-retirement continues. Numerous portrait drawings, very delicately drawn, many lightly washed with yellow; including the portrait of MRS ERIC KENNINGTON, now in the Fitzwilliam Museum, Cambridge. The Tate Gallery PORTRAIT OF MISS EDITH SITWELL (Pl. 37, note p. 96) was begun this year, not completed until 1935.

1924   Semi-retirement continues. Further portrait drawings, also numerous abstractions in pen, ink and wash. (Examples reproduced in *The Tyro*, No. 2.)

PUBLICATIONS

The Tyro, Nos. 1 and 2. Edited by Wyndham Lewis. The Egoist Press. A Review of the arts of Painting, Sculpture and Design. No. 1 appeared in folio size with a thin paper cover bearing a drawing by the artist. It included, among others, literary contributions by T. S. Eliot, Herbert Read, John Rodker and Wyndham Lewis; and reproductions of the work of David Bomberg, Frank Dobson, William Roberts and Wyndham Lewis (three examples). No. 2 appeared bound as a magazine also with a drawing by the artist on the cover. It contained, among others, literary contributions by T. S. Eliot, Jessie Dismorr, Herbert Read, Waldemar George, and Wyndham Lewis; and reproductions of work by Jessie Dismorr, Frank Dobson, Frederick Etchells, Cedric Morris, Edward Wadsworth and Wyndham Lewis (six examples). A large collection of material related to these publications—

corrected typescripts, page- and galley-proofs and some unpublished matter—is in the Carlow Collection.

1925   Semi-retirement continues. Few examples survive of numerous pen, ink and wash abstractions like BIRD AND FIGURE (Pl. 7, note p. 86).

1926   Further examples in pen, ink and wash (including THE SIBYL reproduced in *The Enemy*, No. 1). Period of retirement ends with the General Strike. The beginning of a period of intense literary work.
PUBLICATION
The Art of Being Ruled, Chatto and Windus. Corrected typescripts, page-proofs and some autograph manuscript material are in the Carlow collection.

1927   Further abstractions in pen, ink and wash including THE PILLAR (Pl. 6, note p. 85). Other examples reproduced in *The Enemy*, Nos. 1 and 2.
PUBLICATIONS
The Enemy, Nos. 1 and 2, edited by Wyndham Lewis, the Arthur Press. A review of art and literature. Published January and September, respectively. No. 1 contained reproductions of a picture by Chirico and six drawings by Wyndham Lewis including FIGURES IN THE AIR in colour. No. 2 contained the first version of PALEFACE and reproductions of two drawings by Wyndham Lewis. The covers of both numbers designed and lettered by the artist. Corrected typescripts, page- and galley-proofs, etc., connected with both numbers, are in the Carlow collection.

    The Lion and the Fox, Grant Richards. Typescripts, page-proofs, etc., are in the Carlow collection.

    Time and Western Man, Chatto and Windus. Including The Revolutionary Simpleton (Book 1) and An Analysis of the Philosophy of Time (Book 2). Book 1 formed the major contribution to *The Enemy* No. 1. Corrected typescripts, page- and galley-proofs, with a large quantity of holograph manuscript material, are in the Carlow collection.

    The Wild Body, Chatto and Windus. Containing 'A Soldier of Humour' and other stories. Also published in a special edition of seventy-nine copies, with six complimentary copies, all signed by the author. Several of the stories appeared in *The Little Review* during 1917 and 1918, 'Sigismund' appeared in *Art and Letters* during 1920. Copies of these magazines, containing a number of the stories, are in the Carlow collection; together with corrected typescripts and page-proofs of the book.

1928   Few examples survive. The semi-abstract pen and ink drawing SENTINELS (Pl. 8, note p. 86) was reproduced in *The Enemy*, No. 3.

BAGDAD: A PANEL (Pl. 9, note p. 86) is the first in a major series of semi-abstract oil-paintings chiefly produced in the 'thirties.

PUBLICATIONS

The Childermass, Vol. 1, Chatto and Windus. Also published in a special edition of 225 copies, with six for private distribution, all signed by the author. This was originally planned as a longer work but volume 2 was not completed. Corrected typescripts, page- and galley-proofs, etc., with material for volume 2, are in the Carlow collection.

Tarr, Chatto and Windus. A new edition, very extensively revised, for the Phoenix Library. Some material connected with this edition is in the Carlow collection.

1929 Abstractions in pen, ink and wash. BEACH SCENE (Pl. 14, note p. 88) is one of a series of ten or twelve commissioned drawings representing different kinds of sport. The dust wrapper for *The Apes of God* designed this year (Pl. 11, note p. 87).

PUBLICATIONS

The Enemy, No. 3, edited by Wyndham Lewis. The Arthur Press. With reproductions of three pen and ink drawings (see note above, 1928), one repeated in two sizes (with lettering) on front cover; also a pen and ink drawing on back cover.

Paleface: The Philosophy of the Melting Pot, Chatto and Windus. Dust wrapper designed and lettered by the artist. Some material relating to the first version of *Paleface* (as it appeared in *The Enemy*, No. 2) is in the Carlow collection. (See p. 41.)

1930 Portrait drawings in pencil and wash.

PUBLICATIONS

The Apes of God, The Arthur Press. A subscription edition of 750 copies, all signed by the author. With reproductions of fifteen pen and ink drawings. Dust wrapper designed and partially lettered by Wyndham Lewis. (See note above, 1929.) Corrected typescripts, page-proofs, etc., together with numerous sketches and several drawings for this publication, are in the Carlow collection.

Satire and Fiction, The Arthur Press. *Enemy* pamphlet, No. 1, containing 'The History of a Rejected Review' (of *The Apes of God*) by Roy Campbell. Paper cover with a device by Wyndham Lewis. Similar in format to *The Tyro*, No. 1. Some typescript and other material relating to this publication is in the Carlow collection.

1931 Drawings in pencil and wash, including several of a Sealyham dog.

PUBLICATIONS

The Diabolical Principle and The Dithyrambic Spectator, Chatto and Windus. With a design on the dust wrapper and half-title page by Wyndham Lewis (also reproduced on front cover of *The Enemy*, No. 3).

Hitler, Chatto and Windus. Illustrated with photographs not of the artist's work. Dust wrapper designed and lettered by Wyndham Lewis.

1932   Numerous drawings in pencil. Those reproduced in *Thirty Person-alities* (and which formed the exhibition towards the end of the year) were all made in July and August. The drawing MRS DESMOND HARMSWORTH (Pl. 34, note p. 95) is a typical example of this well-known series.

The beginning of a period of illness lasting intermittently for five years.

EXHIBITION

In October, at the Lefevre Galleries (then in King Street), Wyndham Lewis held his third exhibition, 'Thirty Personalities'. Fine pencil drawings similar to the example reproduced, chiefly of celebrated men and women, including G. K. Chesterton, Father D'Arcy, Augustus John, Edith Evans, Rebecca West.

PUBLICATIONS

The Apes of God, Nash and Grayson. A cheap edition, in smaller format, photographically reproduced from the edition of 1930. Illustrations and dust wrapper as in former edition.

The Doom of Youth, Chatto and Windus. Corrected typescript in the Carlow collection.

The Enemy of the Stars, Desmond Harmsworth. Including 'Physics of the Not-Self', an essay. The title-play is a revised edition of the version in *Blast*, No. 1. With reproductions of four drawings, one repeated on the dust wrapper where it is surrounded by another mask-head, both over-printed in colour. On the cover, another head. Corrected typescripts, galley-proofs, etc., in the Carlow collection.

Filibusters in Barbary, Grayson and Grayson. A record of a visit to the Sous. Corrected typescript in the Carlow collection.

Snooty Baronet, Cassell.

Thirty Personalities and a Self-Portrait, Desmond Harmsworth. Reproductions in a folio of the portrait drawings shown at the exhibition; with the addition of the pen drawing of James Joyce made in 1920.

1933   The onset of a very productive period of varied work culminating in the exhibitions of 1937 and 1938. Side by side with the portraits, and in the same category as BAGDAD: A PANEL, of 1928 (Pl. 9, note p. 86), numerous semi-abstract oil paintings from the following years gradually formed a major series in the artist's highly individual mixed-idiom (of naturalism and abstraction, see note p. 54). For reasons connected with the exhibition of 1937, dates on the pictures and dates of completion do not always correspond. Thus BEACH BABIES, for example

(Pl. 13, note p. 88), dated 1933, was not in fact completed until 1936. A later date of completion is also presumed for RED SCENE,[1] Tate Gallery, though it, too, is dated 1933.

Besides paintings in oil, numerous abstractions in pen and wash, also several drawings in pencil and wash.

PUBLICATIONS

The Old Gang and the New, Desmond Harmsworth.

One Way Song, Faber and Faber. Containing the title-poem and 'Engine Fight Talk', 'The Song of the Militant Romance', 'If So the Man You Are', and 'Envoi'. With five designs by the artist. Also published in an edition limited to forty signed and numbered copies. Corrected typescripts, galley-proofs and holograph manuscript material, together with six designs for the book, in the Carlow collection.

1934   Further work towards the exhibition of 1937, chiefly semi-abstracts in oil and in pen, ink and wash.

PUBLICATION

Men Without Art, Cassell. Corrected typescripts, galley-proofs and some holograph manuscript material in the Carlow collection.

1935   Besides work for the exhibition, the whole series of drawings for *Beyond This Limit* was made in this year; and the Tate Gallery PORTRAIT OF MISS EDITH SITWELL, begun in 1933 (Pl. 37, note p. 96), was completed. Other examples include various life drawings in pencil and wash.

PUBLICATIONS

Beyond This Limit, Jonathan Cape. Pictures by Wyndham Lewis, words by Naomi Mitchison. With thirty pen and ink drawings, one reproduced on the dust wrapper.

(*The Roaring Queen*, completed this year, was withdrawn before publication.)

1936   Examples of each mode in all media. Among the oils, THE SURRENDER OF BARCELONA (Pl. 16, note p. 89), Tate Gallery, also BLACK AND RED PRINCIPLE. BEACH BABIES (Pl. 13, note p. 88) and THE CONVALESCENT (Colour Plate C, note p. 83) were both completed this year, though dated 1933. Also numerous portrait drawings, chiefly of the artist's wife, including WOMAN IN AN ARMCHAIR (Pl. 38, note p. 96), and READING, a similar example in the British Museum (note p. 96).

PUBLICATION

Left Wings over Europe: or How to Make a War About Nothing, Jonathan Cape.

1937   Further varied examples. THE ARMADA (Pl. 17, note p. 89) also two undated abstractions, MUD CLINIC (Pl. 28, note p. 93) and PLAYERS

---

[1] Reproduced in *Emporium*, vol. 105, April 1947, p. 169 (as Scena Rossa).

ON THE STAGE (Pl. 20, note p. 90). Like BEACH BABIES, above, the STATIONS OF THE DEAD (Pl. 19, note p. 90) was completed this year though dated 1933. Portraits in oil for which the artist's wife sat as model include FROANNA, Glasgow Art Gallery, and the RED PORTRAIT (Pl. 41, note p. 98).

EXHIBITION

In December, the fourth exhibition, the second at the Leicester Galleries: twenty-four paintings and thirty-four drawings from the work of the past seven years. A Foreword in the catalogue by the artist. Outstanding among those pictures not so far quoted (and not reproduced) were: PORTRAIT OF MISS MARGARET ANNE BOWES-LYON, MASQUERADE IN A LANDSCAPE, NEWFOUNDLAND and QUEUE OF THE DEAD.

PUBLICATIONS

Blasting and Bombardiering, Eyre and Spottiswoode (Autobiography, 1914–26). With reproductions of twelve portrait heads, four pen and wash abstractions and four photographs. Dust wrapper with devices by Wyndham Lewis. Page-proofs and corrected galley-proofs in the Carlow collection.

Count Your Dead: They Are Alive! Lovat Dickson. With two designs on the dust wrapper, one repeated on the title-page. Corrected typescript, galley-proofs and a large quantity of holograph manuscript material in the Carlow collection.

The Revenge for Love, Cassell. Corrected typescripts, with a large quantity of manuscript material, some unpublished, in the Carlow collection.

1938   A series of important portraits and numerous related portrait studies in pencil and chalk. The following, here reproduced, were shown at the summer exhibition and subsequently acquired by public institutions: the 'first' PORTRAIT OF T. S. ELIOT (Pl. 40, note p. 97), Durban Art Gallery, South Africa; the PORTRAIT OF MRS T. J. HONEYMAN (Pl. 36, note p. 96), Glasgow Art Gallery; and the PORTRAIT OF STEPHEN SPENDER (Pl. 42, note p. 98), Public Art Gallery, Hanley. Also completed this year but not exhibited were LA SUERTE and the PORTRAIT OF EZRA POUND (Pl. 47, note p. 100), now both in the Tate Gallery (see also the sketch HEAD OF EZRA POUND, Pl. 46, note p. 99). The PORTRAIT OF JOHN MACLEOD (Pl. 48, note p. 100), and the PORTRAIT OF NAOMI MITCHISON (Pl. 43, note p. 98) were also included in the exhibition.

Abstractions in oil include the FOUR FIGURE COMPOSITION (Pl. 23, note p. 91).

EXHIBITION

In July, at the Beaux Arts Gallery, Bruton Place, the fifth exhibition 'New Paintings and Drawings': seven portraits, eight abstractions in oil, twelve drawings.

PUBLICATION

The Mysterious Mr Bull, Robert Hale. Corrected typescripts, galley-proofs, etc., with a large quantity of holograph manuscript material, in the Carlow collection.

1939 Further examples in the series of portraits and portrait-studies including the PORTRAIT OF MISS CLOSE and the PORTRAIT OF A SMILING GENTLEMAN. The PORTRAIT OF JULIAN SYMONS, begun this year, was completed in 1949.

PUBLICATIONS

The Jews, Are They Human? G. Allen and Unwin.

The Hitler Cult, Dent.

Wyndham Lewis the Artist: from Blast to Burlington House, Laidlaw and Laidlaw. Including reproductions of three paintings in colour, six half-tone and three designs in black and white.

1940–8 During the war years, a long visit to Canada and the U.S.A. Despite acute personal difficulties Wyndham Lewis continued his work as an artist and author, occasionally sending in to exhibitions, also lecturing. The large body of work then produced is now widely distributed among private collectors, Colleges, Museums and Art Galleries. Very few examples have so far been seen in England.

Examples of portraits in oils include the PORTRAIT OF DR JOSEPH ERLANGER (Nobel Prize Winner), now in the Medical Schools at Washington University, U.S.A.; the PORTRAIT OF MRS HENRY MARTIN, Windsor, Ontario; and the PORTRAIT OF J. S. MACLEAN in the sitter's private collection, Toronto. A series of portrait drawings made in 1945 is recorded in the Museum of Modern Art, New York.

A series of pen and ink abstractions was made on the theme of the European War. LEBENSRAUM: THE BATTLEFIELD is now in the Art Gallery of Toronto. Other examples in pen and ink include ALLEGRESSE AQUATIQUE (Pl. 24, note p. 92) in the Art Gallery, Toronto; also GARGOYLES and WITCHES SURPRISED AT DAWN, both in the J. S. MacLean collection, Toronto; and JUPITER THE THUNDERER, MARINE FIESTA, WITCH ON COW BACK and BATHING WOMEN, all in the collection of Douglas Duncan, Toronto. NEGRO HEAVEN, 1946, was the only example from the war years exhibited at the Redfern Gallery Retrospective Exhibition in 1949; now in the City Art Gallery, Glasgow.

Wyndham Lewis returned to England in 1948. LYNETTE (Pl. 45, note p. 99) is typical of various life-studies made in this year.

CHRONOLOGICAL OUTLINE

PUBLICATIONS

1940. *America, I Presume*, Soskins, New York.

1941. *The Vulgar Streak*, Robert Hale.

1942. *Anglosaxony*, Ryerson Press, Toronto.

1948. *America and Cosmic Man*, Nicholson and Watson.

1949   Varied work, all examples quoted being shown at the exhibition. Among the oil-paintings the 'second' PORTRAIT OF T. S. ELIOT (Pl. B, note p. 82), and the PORTRAIT OF JULIAN SYMONS (begun in 1939), also the semi-abstract THE ROOM THAT MARY LIVES IN were completed this year.

The abstractions in pen, ink and wash were characterized by bright colours, complex designs and figures closely woven into the surrounding detail as in THE ASCENT, THE GEOGRAPHER and WHAT THE SEA IS LIKE AT NIGHT (Pl. 25, note p. 92).

A third autobiographical volume was written this year under the title *Rude Assignment*.[1]

EXHIBITION[2]

In May, at the Redfern Gallery, the 'Retrospective Exhibition'. One hundred drawings and twenty-one paintings were shown. (A few items listed in the catalogue were either not sent or not hung.) The exhibits represented the artist's work between 1909 and 1949, many being lent by private collectors. Important drawings made between 1911 and 1921 were sent from the Rutherston Collection. Michael Ayrton wrote a Foreword and Wyndham Lewis an Introduction for the illustrated catalogue. The exhibition was organized by Rex Nan Kivell.

[1] Published by Hutchinson, November 1950.

[2] In February 1950, an exhibition of thirty-one water-colour drawings by Wyndham Lewis was held at Victoria College, Toronto. All the items exhibited dated from 1941, 1942 and 1943. Organized by Mr Douglas Duncan of Toronto the exhibition ran for three weeks. Several of the works quoted above were shown, including ALLEGRESSE AQUATIQUE (Pl. 24), on loan from the Toronto Art Gallery.

3

Detail in the Style of Wyndham Lewis

by

CHARLES HANDLEY-READ

D. DRAGON IN A CAGE

1

Imaginative Compositions

In his essay on Wyndham Lewis, Mr Eric Newton has discussed the artist within the large context of the twentieth century. His aim, if I read him correctly, is to indicate the importance of Wyndham Lewis's contribution to the art of the present day in this country. In his placing of the artist, and by his most interesting use of comparisons, Mr Newton has shown the approach both of the critic and the art historian; and in each capacity he has necessarily been concerned, for the most part, with broad statements. In what follows I shall, by contrast, discuss examples of Wyndham Lewis's work at close range, attempting to fulfil the function of a lens. My aim is to reveal certain details of style and technique; and thereby to assist those as yet unfamiliar with it towards an intimate appreciation of the artist's achievements.

But it is impossible to study detail in an artist's work without reference to a very large number of examples. The number of reproductions in this book being limited, references to certain examples not reproduced here are inevitable, though these have been reduced to a minimum; and they are, in fact, confined to work previously reproduced in the artist's own publications. Descriptions of detail are throughout related to specific examples.

EARLY WORK

In the art of Wyndham Lewis recurring traits of style identify the artist as emphatically as a signature, despite a variety of different modes of expression. Easily recognized characteristics appear in the group of over twenty drawings from the year 1912, the first large surviving body of his work. Here, at once, we are in the presence of power and ability.

One series, typified by TWO FIGURES (Pl. 1), represents a primitive world inhabited by elemental creatures, inarticulate men and women from the cave. In some examples the figures appear like statues carved from the living rock, their arms and legs following the natural lines of the strata. Sculptural and archaic, with jagged torsos, heavy thighs and the knees of oxen, the skulls of all the figures are hacked irregularly away above the forehead. The eyes are

51

large, unseeing, tokens of a sense which does not yet fulfil its proper function. Character is emphasized by impulsive draughtsmanship and deeply scored lines. The impression of savage power thus created is in contrast to the earth-warm colours, soft brown and mushroom pink, of the background scenes. Grouped in pairs, they struggle to raise boulders from the ground, attempt to communicate with each other, gaze blindly at a world which they will never understand. In a moon-landscape of rocks and flickering light, yearning, desolate, frustrated, they evoke pity as they perform their tragic rites.

In another series of pen and ink drawings, touched, here and there, with vivid colours, the figures are represented by the sharp, incisive lines that are to become, from now on, a very important feature in Wyndham Lewis's work. The figures move violently, perhaps in a dance, often against angular backgrounds. A hectic vitality supersedes the resignation of the men and women of the caves. The once-rugged faces are now simian, negroid, displaying a cruel smile, shrewd eyes and the sophisticated mystery of a theatrical mask; for the dancers belong to the stage and they are illuminated by flood-lights. THE CENTAURESS (Pl. 5) is one of the primitive figures but she stands against an angular background, like a drop-cloth, a background heralding Vorticism.

VORTICISM

This movement was invented, sustained and developed by Wyndham Lewis between 1912 and 1915. Though it attracted many followers it is best defined by him and with reference to his own work. 'Vorticism,' he wrote in 1939, 'accepted the machine world: that is the point to stress. It sought out machine forms. The pictures of the Vorticists were a sort of machine. . . . It was cheerfully and dogmatically external. . . .'[1] It was a movement militating against Impressionism (and Futurism) and it culminated in the series of 'Plans' and 'Planners' and with the 'Timon' drawings of its founder.

A 'vortex' is defined in the dictionary as a 'system that swallows up those who approach it'. This definition applies precisely to several of the drawings in the Timon series where the mechanical aspect of the style is also clearly demonstrated (see example, Pl. 3, note p. 84). Here, in a seemingly chaotic design, made up of cubes and segments of masonry, and bristling with struts and spars, a number of overseeing Robots appear to be engaged in work of super-human reconstruction. A glaring white light casts dark shadows, reveals surprising detail. Razor-sharp lines define the angles, the geometric curves, the arrogant Robots themselves. The design is organized so that it suggests the view seen when looking up into a pylon from below: there is an effect in the drawing of hurtling perspective, of far-reaching recession among bars and angles. In several of the Timon drawings it is as if the onlooker is about to be drawn up towards

[1] *Wyndham Lewis the Artist: from Blast to Burlington House*, p. 78.

a point near the top of the picture, the focus or vortex into which the Robots themselves, despite their confidence, seem bound to follow.

Unlike the thinly washed drawings of the Timon series, most of the 'Plans' and 'Planners' were painted in gouache. Monochromatic examples in black and white alternate with those built up in strips of very bright colour. In both groups the major lines appear to extend radially from a focal point of disturbance which is, once again, the vortex. After saying of one particular example that 'THE PLANNERS (Pl. 4) is a *title*, merely, found for the purposes of exhibition', the artist gives the following account of this and similar drawings: 'The way those things were done . . . is that a mental-emotive impulse—and by this is meant subjective intellection, like magic or religion—is let loose upon a lot of blocks and lines of various dimensions, and encouraged to push them round and to arrange them at will. It is of course not an accidental, isolated mood: but it is recurrent groups of emotions and coagulations of thinking that is involved.'[1]

In several examples the outlines of a figure are imposed upon the plan. In others no figures appear and the significance of these drawings lies in the fact that they are completely abstract, pure systems of lines and shapes without representational content of any kind. At the beginning of the first world war *total* abstraction was rare, even on the Continent; and that it now appeared in England, in the work of the Vorticists, was due entirely to the invention and foresight of Wyndham Lewis. There was at this time an urgent need for experiment in art. Mr Newton has discussed the effect of the manifestos, and the importance of the artist's aims and work of the *Blast* period. The 'Plans' and 'Planners' represent a climax in Wyndham Lewis's early career; for with their 'musical-abstract symbols' they demonstrate perfectly that 'divorce from external, sensuous reality' which he was then determined to achieve. They also occupy an important place in the history of English art. It was by means of these early abstracts that he attempted, as he has recently expressed it, 'to hustle the cultural Britannia'.[2]

Vorticism was abandoned by Wyndham Lewis when he joined the Army in 1915. The work of 1917 and 1918 records clearly and powerfully certain visual aspects of war, acutely observed by an artist who came upon the scene with '. . . one or other of the attendant genii of passion at his elbow, exciting him to make his work a *work of action*'.[3] Animated, formalized, naturalistic, the war scenes show the subtle and appropriate use of many shapes and idioms invented for Vorticism. For a discussion of A BATTERY SHELLED (Pl. 26), the only war-picture reproduced in this book—and mentioned here for the sake of chronological continuity—the reader may be referred to Mr Newton's essay (p. 21).

[1] From a letter to the Editor, September 1949.

[2] Catalogue Foreword, R.G.R.E., 1949.

[3] Catalogue Foreword to the Goupil Gallery Exhibition 'Guns', 1919.

DETAIL IN THE STYLE OF WYNDHAM LEWIS
LATER ABSTRACTIONS

The whole of Wyndham Lewis's work since the 1914–18 war may be divided into two categories of roughly equal numerical content: the paintings and drawings from life and the imaginative compositions here under discussion. Among the latter, during the early 'twenties, new forms, new idioms appeared. Discussing the difference between the Vorticist method of total abstraction and the 'literary' method exemplified in the post-war examples, the artist says that '. . . on the musical-abstract symbols of 1914 the emotive intellect is let loose (though under some control) upon a multitude of blocks and lines, and composes its own fugue'; but when, on the other hand, '. . . the *literary imagination* is invited to compose—in a highly selective but far more complex world of forms, usually dominated by one colour . . . ', the result is then a work in the 'mixed idiom of *pure-abstraction-and-stylized-nature*'.[1] The artist has also described examples in the mixed-idiom as those '. . . independent abstractions that suggest themselves as a result of any observation of nature that is at all profound'.[2]

The first abstractions in the mixed idiom appeared in 1921. A long series in this genre has grown regularly since that date and is represented by Plate numbers 6 to 25. The series includes designs and illustrations in pen, ink and wash, a number of 'dream' pictures; historical and architectural fantasies and visions; satirical works; and what may be called metaphysical speculations. An astonishing variety is at once apparent, yet variety does not obscure a relationship between each example. The relationship, apart from technique, lies in the stylization of the subject, whatever it may be, into the form of absolutely personal idioms and symbols. The common factor in each picture is a figure. Sometimes the figure (or group of figures) is a symbol of something else to be interpreted in a literary context; sometimes the figure or group is a formal, imaginative creation existing in its own right and without 'meaning'. To ask the meaning of the symbols—apart from the context in which they appear, if they have one—or to ask why the symbols assume the form they do, is tantamount to asking why Mr Wyndham Lewis is what he is; and of course the question is unanswerable. As Mr Newton has suggested, the symbols are some kind of equivalent, in concrete forms, of unconscious life; and here it is impossible for me to proceed any farther. It is even very difficult to say what some of the pictures 'mean' in literary terms, and it is certainly impossible to generalize on their meanings; though it may be possible to indicate lines of interpretation when faced, later, with certain individual examples. Meanwhile, whatever may be the origin and meaning of the symbols, or the meaning of the paintings and drawings, the fact that every example in the mixed idiom contains a figure is sufficient reason for subjecting the figures to an analysis in

[1] From a letter to the Editor, September 1949.

[2] *Wyndham Lewis the Artist*, p. 59.

terms of appearance. Infinitely varied, the figures are among Wyndham Lewis's most important inventions; and if a frieze of all the figures could be formed it would be seen that he has created a variety, a species, almost, that is unique in art.

We shall see later that in a discussion of the life drawings the outline is of paramount importance. With the abstracted figures, the emphasis goes on the shapes and on the infilling. But one characteristic of the life drawings is carried over into the mixed idiom and that is the sense of pose. Lightly petalled or heavily plated, lapped in the shapes of flames or blocked and seamed like sculpture in leather: whether still or animated the stance or action of the figures is so perfectly characterized that pose alone disarms inquiry as to the purpose of their being, the exact nature of their activity. A deep feeling for anatomy and the structure of the human body enables Wyndham Lewis to load his figures, to build them up, in numerous examples, in a kind of metallic carapace; yet they are always able to move freely and gracefully. A group of plated figures flies out diagonally, beautifully poised, at the top of the pole in FIGURES IN THE AIR[1]; and at the base of the pole the dead '*héros allongé*' suggests, by pose alone, an action of fruitless self-sacrifice. The left-hand figure in BEACH SCENE (Pl. 14), partially plated and decorated with rosettes, has all the grace, the same S bend and yet something of the angularity of a Gothic Madonna. Even when clothed in full armour, as in the SURRENDER OF BARCELONA (Pl. 16) and ARMADA (Pl. 17), the figures are still able to gesticulate with ease, walk lightly, and demonstrate by their actions a human form below the weight of metal.

There are also the skeletal figures of A TANK IN THE CLINIC,[2] the shop-window lay figures of the MUD CLINIC (Pl. 21), the figures cut from cardboard in the STATIONS OF THE DEAD (Pl. 19); and there are the metamorphic figures of BIRD AND FIGURE (Pl. 7), for example, in which the shapes of birds, and even of fishes, merge imperceptibly into human form. Again and again the pose or stance, based on that of human models, lends validity to the figures whatever the forms they may combine, whatever the nature of the person represented. An extreme and silent dignity is seen in the standing women of FOUR FIGURE COMPOSITION (Pl. 23). Authority is suggested by the erect posture of the halo'd God in DAWN IN EREWHON.[3] And in the BEACH BABIES (Pl. 13), the pert expression, set to catch the camera-man, is emphasized by the pose which is the satirical epitome of coquettishness at the seaside. Heroic and monumental, frail and pathetic, the figures of Gods and giants and angels alternate with cavemen,

---

[1] Reproduced in colour in *The Enemy*, No. 1, opposite p. 14. Exhibited R.G.R.E., No. 94, as ON THE ROOF. Details on p. 86.

[2] Reproduced in colour in *Pavilion*, edited by Myfanwy Evans, p. 8, accompanying an article by Wyndham Lewis: 'Towards an Earth Culture'.

[3] Reproduced in *Blasting and Bombardiering* between pp. 216 and 217.

gladiators, dancers; creatures of heaven and earth, a fantastic parade of the quick, the dead and the damned. But the catalogue of shapes and forms is not yet complete. Among the most interesting figures are those resembling a totem pole.

The totem motif has appealed to Wyndham Lewis at all times. One of the first post-Vorticist abstractions, the COLUMN FIGURES[1] of 1921, shows two finely chiselled blocks of wood, inevitably recalling the poles of the Chilkat country. Of very recent date (1949) there is THE GEOGRAPHER,[2] a design arranged up the page so that the whole drawing resembles a totem pole, though it is not intended to represent one. Numerous drawings of the ENEMY period (ROMAN ACTORS, Pl. 15, MAGELLAN, SUNSET ATLAS[3]) show the whole paraphernalia of mask-heads, obtruding limbs, and tight, horizontal detail arranged in strata as the columns rise. Again, a vertical arrangement of detail, in horizontal sections, is seen in the two figures on the right-hand side of BAGDAD: A PANEL (Pl. 9). Totemic patterns—imbricated fillets and edges, masks and bird helmets—appear too often for individual quotation. But in spite of the physical detail and the soaring verticality of the designs as a whole, these totem figures are inanimate. Inevitably deprived of the opportunity to indulge in pose or gesture, they are for this reason in a category by themselves among the abstracted figures of the mixed-idiom. They make their impact through pattern and detail and by the hint of magic with which, by association, they are endowed.

In the drawings from life, as we shall see later, Wyndham Lewis pays particular attention to the hands of his sitters. And mailed hands and fingers, and the outline shapes of hands, may be found in THE ARMADA (Pl. 17), in the SURRENDER OF BARCELONA (Pl. 16), in FIGURES IN THE AIR, and in BEACH SCENE (Pl. 14).[4] But it is an interesting feature of the abstractions—both the paintings and drawings—that hands and feet are usually suppressed. The hands are either buried in drapery, or they are hidden by what they hold, or, through ingenuity of posing, they are made to disappear round a body so that they are not seen. Very often the arms and legs are tapered away, but so elegantly and unobtrusively that their absence is not at once noticed. There are also examples in which the arms and legs are deliberately truncated (BEACH BABIES, Pl. 13, STATIONS OF THE DEAD, Pl. 19); while there are numerous figures which appear simply as a torso with a head, when the addition of hands and feet would be out of the question. This suppression of hands and feet is of course deliberate. Their

[1] Exhibited R.G.R.E., No. 5.

[2] Exhibited R.G.R.E., No. 44.

[3] MAGELLAN was reproduced in *The Enemy*, No. 1, opposite p. viii. SUNSET ATLAS was reproduced in *Wyndham Lewis the Artist*, p. 352.

[4] Hands and clenched or mailed fists may also be found among the illustrations to *The Apes of God* and *One Way Song*.

inclusion would interfere, very often, with the grace and simplicity of the pose, the impression of fluid movement; they would hinder the quick grasp of essential forms which the stylization of the figures is partly designed to encourage; and finally, in many cases, the inclusion of hands and feet (for hands, in particular, are very apt to betray personality) would conflict with the enigmatic nature of the figure-symbols. In any case, all we need to know about the figures is conveyed by pose and by the character and expression of the heads. And like the bodies, the heads are worthy of analysis and a catalogue.

Examples of 'pin-heads' are first seen in a series of drawings of 1912—surely a very early appearance of a species now found in the work of several contemporary artists and sculptors.[1] In these drawings a small head, like a pea, is raised on the neck which acts as a pedestal, the neck being supported, in turn, upon a gigantic torso. In the Timon series of the pre-Vorticist period there were the helmeted heads of the Robots. Now, in more recent times, the 'pin-head' species is further developed and varied. There are, for example, the turnip-heads of the INFERNO, where the dead and glassy eyes are like bulbs or marbles pressed into the vegetable flesh. In other examples we see the slit eyes and grinning mouths of heads resembling lanterns prepared for Hallowe'en. A wig is added to a ball of wood—and we have the gracious ladies of FOUR FIGURE COMPOSITION (Pl. 23). Two discs are put in below the chiselled eye-brow lines—and we see the hopeless resignation of the waiting figures in MUD CLINIC (Pl. 21). Then, in a different style, there are the 'loud-speaker' heads first appearing in one of the designs for *Beyond This Limit*. Related to them, the mechanical man in PLAYERS ON THE STAGE (Pl. 20) has a box-like head with a megaphone for a mouth. In a drawing of the 'twenties, ROOM NO. 55,[2] there are several heads drawn as though they were cut from sheet metal, resembling the sculpture of Gargallo. Other metallic heads include those sharpened and compressed into the shapes of shells and bullets, usually belonging to the figures in which the plates of the bodies are identified with the muscles. But the 'pin-heads' are the most common—round heads like footballs, punch-balls, turnips, lanterns; flat discs of cardboard—and after these come the heads and faces in the form of a mask.

Like the pin-headed figures, faces in the form of a mask first appeared in 1912.[3] Whether, in most examples, there is a head inside the mask, or whether the mask actually represents the head (when a symbolic significance may be intended), it is sometimes difficult to say. But both masks and mask-heads appear, as we have seen, in the stratified lines of decoration of the totem figures.

[1] 'Pin-head' figures are found in THE DOMINO and COURTSHIP, both of 1912, in the Baker Collection, V&AM. Similar figures are found in drawings of 1913 in the same collection and in the drawing POST JAZZ, reproduced in the Ovid Press folio of *Fifteen Drawings*.

[2] Reproduced in *The Tyro*, No. 2, iii.

[3] As in KERMESSE, exhibited R.G.R.E., No. 11, reproduced in *Blast*, No. 1, p. 74.

A classical mask-head appears with the head of a horse in *Beyond This Limit*[1]; a figure with a Japanese mask rides a horse on the cover of the *Enemy* (No. 3); and a related drawing called, simply, THE ENEMY,[2] shows a figure with two masks surmounting an enormous torso. Of the same period, a figure at the top of the pole in the drawing on the back of the *Enemy* (No. 3) is also mask-headed; and in this example the classical face is surmounted by curling hair, low and flat on the forehead. The same treatment of the classical mask-head, where the hair is arranged to hide the absence of the top of the skull, is found in BAGDAD: A PANEL (Pl. 9). (It will be remembered that the truncated skull is a feature of the drawings of 1912.) And again, in several drawings of the *Enemy* period the heads are formed from exaggerated eye-masks in the Venetian style. Finally, there are the armour-masks which decorate the title-page of *One Way Song*; and there are the 'primitive' masks decorating the cover and several pages of *The Enemy of the Stars*.

In his symbols, and for his motifs, Wyndham Lewis also draws extensively on the animal world. Tigers and horses, pigs and black swans—brassy, heraldic, exquisitely drawn—all are to be found in *Beyond This Limit*. Two horse-like animals also appear in the DRAWING FOR JONATHAN SWIFT[3] and here the shovel-shaped heads, at the end of necks like drain-pipes, with their alternately scoured-out and rounded forms, remind one of the sculpture of Ossip Zadkine. Among the animals, it is perhaps unnecessary to mention the terrifying simian form appearing on the cover of *The Apes of God*: this at least is well known. But there are also innumerable creatures of mixed species, zoomorphs in which the forms proper to the inhabitants of land, sea and air are moulded together; they are seen in several incidental drawings of the *Enemy* period, and in numerous decorations for *The Apes of God*. The Centauresses of the early drawings should also be recalled at this point. What is remarkable about the treatment of all these creatures is their convincing animality. It seems very likely that at some point in his career Wyndham Lewis must have spent long hours at a zoo, studying the carriage and form of many different beasts, making and probably destroying many life-studies. None appear to survive, but the evidence of very careful observation may be seen whenever the form of a horse finds its way into one of the pictures.[4]

[1] p. 47.

[2] *Wyndham Lewis the Artist*, opposite p. 240.

[3] Reproduced in *The Tyro*, No. 2, viii.

[4] While correcting proofs, a drawing (*c.* 1912) has come into my possession similar to those in the series typified by SUNSET AMONG THE MICHELANGELOS, Baker Collection, V&AM. In my drawing the central figure in a group of three holds reins securing two horses forming part of the background. One of the horses' heads, drawn as a flat silhouette, has a mask attached to it—a kind of parody of a horse-head in mask form—so that the horse appears to be double-headed. A further point of interest is the treatment of the horse's mane (indicated by a white strip), where black lines are apparently arranged to resemble the grouping of the black keys of a piano.

While the drawings in the mixed idiom are not so important, considered as a body of work, as the oil-paintings in the same category, we have seen that they contain a variety of delightful and interesting inventions. One of the most fascinating aspects of the drawings is the actual technique of pen-draughtsmanship. The line is lithe and sharp, perfectly controlled, struck off spontaneously in scimitar curves with complete confidence. But it is within the areas defined by the line that the invention and versatility of draughtsmanship are most remarkable. It is perfectly obvious that with pen in hand, and with a clean sheet of paper before him, Wyndham Lewis can settle down to enjoy himself. Neither invention nor technique ever seem to fail. Looking at THE SENTINELS, for example (Pl. 8), at BEACH SCENE (Pl. 14), at MAGELLAN or at any of the drawings for *Beyond This Limit*, it is possible to imagine the artist's procedure at the drawing desk. There are no sketches: if a drawing goes wrong it will be done again, or the faulty area will be cut out, the paper replaced, and the passage re-drawn. There is no scaffolding in pencil: if, for example, a figure is sketched in and later found to be unnecessary, there is no attempt to hide the preliminary lines; they are left, without apology, as it were, and we must ignore them. (See, for example, the 'ghost' figure in the left foreground of BEACH SCENE, Pl. 14.) Watching the artist, we see him draw, first of all, the important horizontal and vertical lines which give a firm basis to the structure of the design. Then, perhaps, the outlines of a group of figures are blocked in, with indications of background detail. We notice that the artist's whole arm is a perfectly trained instrument, the weight of the arm resting on the last joint of the little finger. The finger acts as a kind of ball-bearing runner when the long straight lines are being drawn, and as a pivot or compass point for the curves. Soon, certain areas are precisely hatched in, great care being taken to work up sharp edges, usually on the outer curves of the blade or petal shapes. The shading is graduated, dark to light, within small areas, and variety of texture is gained by fraying out the dark areas so that they fade away in a network of fine lines. But suddenly we realize that with the addition of the heavier shading the essentials of a drawing are there before us: a group of figures with a cavernous background, a totem-pole design, a giant with a frieze of animals . . . and then comes the detail. A little shower of pen strokes, like sun-flower seeds, is stabbed and scattered within the outlines of a building, down the thigh of a leg, across a distant background. Or perhaps a line of dots is delicately pricked in to define the interior modelling of a figure. An even, formal infilling, not too heavy in tone, is required for the angels' heads in the SENTINELS (Pl. 8): and the pen supplies a broken pattern of membranous tissues. In MAGELLAN, a contrast is required to the smooth mask and strong diagonals already marked out; and the flexible nib splays out under considerable pressure making a lovely network of interlacing lines, like a palisade woven in hazel wands. A rich glint is given to one of the animals in *Beyond This Limit* by tight, conventional cross-hatching. For decorative purposes a rosette is added to one of the figures in BEACH SCENE; while many of the drawings are enriched by filigree strips of repetitive ornament. The repetition sets up a rhythm, and the rhythm introduces movement. Some of the patterns seem to belong to the pages of notation for a Ballet. But while many examples are richly and even heavily worked, the areas left blank are often larger and more numerous than those drawn in. In all cases a calculated balance of black and white and a careful regard for negative and positive shapes, help to give the drawings their flickering vitality. When colour is added, a few bright tones lend brilliance to some of the smaller areas—the pennants and maritime buildings in BEACH SCENE, for example—and delicate washes unify the larger areas of background and foreground. The colour reinforces the drawing, sharpens the edges, makes many of the decorative passages glow and twinkle. But colour is subordinated to the tones achieved by ink alone. It is the endless invention of shapes and symbols, the cleanliness of draughtsmanship, the varieties of texture that hold the attention.

But there is no falsity of technique, there are no tricks. At the present time there is a depressing uniformity in many contemporary black and white drawings—those seen, for example, in even the best illustrated books: a kind of neat commercial finish which makes it difficult to tell whether a given example was originally worked out as a wood-cut, a scraper-board drawing, in pen and ink, or even as a lithograph. In Wyndham Lewis's drawings the characteristics proper to pen, ink and paper are not lost but exploited. His shapely lines and calligraphic marquetry are the work of a virtuoso in this medium.

As a designer, Wyndham Lewis could have supplied a fine series of designs for drop-cloths and sets—and the costumes—for a ballet; it is surprising that he has never been asked to do so. As an illustrator, there are half-a-dozen authors, besides Mrs Mitchison and Mr Wyndham Lewis himself, whose visually expressed fantasies could have been interpreted and sustained by his drawings. Nevertheless, his best work in this category will always be that in which we see the promptings of his own unique imagination, the drawings he makes with delight, for his own pleasure.

We have discussed so far the symbols and characters in the paintings and drawings of the mixed idiom, also the artist's technique as a pen-draughtsman. Turning now to the method of composition in the paintings, one feature is immediately striking: the fact that Wyndham Lewis's symbols and backgrounds are presented with an extreme formality of design. Discipline and calculation are, as we shall see later, very strongly marked in the portraits, but in the abstractions and architectural fantasies deliberation over structure is even more rigorous. In every composition there is a rectangularity of design, a tension between rigid vertical and horizontal lines such that each picture seems to be built on a grid or network like a steel frame. It is the immense strength of the straight lines, and the rectangles they form, that give the onlooker confidence. A formal substructure enables Wyndham Lewis to introduce any number of coffee-coloured lay-figures, permits him to record visionary explorations without the danger of a melodramatic result. Theatrical and melodramatic effects, like false surrealist dream pictures (though not, obviously, the early Chirico), are anathema to him. 'Give me the *outside* of all things,'[1] he has said; and his pictures are, in an important sense, fundamentally concrete and physical, externalities being portrayed keenly and without vagueness. Thus when they occur, certain little episodes, and overtones of mood, the unphysical events later to be noted, are all the more surprising within these severely physical worlds where the five senses would seem to be an adequate guide.

Several aspects of the abstractions may be discussed in connection with THE INFERNO.[2] This picture is an example of what I have called a 'metaphysical speculation'. When it was first exhibited at the Leicester Galleries in 1937, Wyndham Lewis wrote in the catalogue: 'In this composition (an inverted T, a vertical red panel and a horizontal grey panel) a world of shapes locked in eternal conflict is superimposed upon a world of shapes, prone in the relaxations of an uneasy sensuality which is also eternal.' This description may be expanded. The 'inverted T' demonstrates perfectly the use of rigid lines of construction which control, in this case, the two panels of writhing figures. The avalanche of damned creatures—red and incandescent in the heat, forming the vertical stroke of the T—is flanked on each side by panels in sick-room green. The panel on the right contains the vertical edge of what might be an open door. Painted pure white, it intensifies the glowing reds of the creatures falling past it. The grey panel across the base of the picture is made up of beings already purged: they are drained of colour, the skin has shrunk to the bone, the eyes start from their sockets. The 'eternal, uneasy sensuality' is tragically evident.

Besides the description of the picture there is another revealing passage in the catalogue foreword. Wyndham Lewis suggests that '. . . it is the function of the artist to translate experience, pleasant and unpleasant, into formal terms. In the latter case,' he continues, 'as what we experience in life is not all pleasant, and the most terrible experience, even, is the most compelling, the result is a tragic picture, as often as not.' To suggest that one particular 'compelling experience' lay behind this picture would, I think, be wrong. More probably THE INFERNO is another example of a process described, it will be remembered, in connection with the pure abstracts of the Vorticist period; a process involving not an 'accidental, isolated mood', but 'recurrent groups of emotions and

---

[1] *Blasting and Bombardiering*, p. 9.

[2] Reproduced in colour in *Wyndham Lewis the Artist*, opposite p. 80. I apologize to the reader for referring so extensively to a picture which in the end it was not possible to reproduce.

coagulations of thinking'. The moods and emotions behind THE INFERNO would be difficult to specify precisely, but the *kinds* of thought may safely be presumed. They are not, after all, so very uncommon. Most people occasionally think of death and dying; we all speculate on the possibility of survival, and the nature of a possible survival, after death; everyone gives anxious thought to his chances of peace beyond the grave. What is unusual is to see thoughts of this kind presented in formal, graphic terms—unusual nowadays, that is: for in the past a Descent of the Damned, a Purgatorial scene, an Inferno, was not so uncommon. And in offering what I believe to be parallel thoughts expressed in a poem, as a kind of interpretation of the picture, I shall not be the first to quote Mr T. S. Eliot in connection with the work of Wyndham Lewis. Besides being another formal presentation of similar metaphysical speculations, the first two verses of the poem 'Whispers of Immortality' contain several lines which exactly describe the figures in the picture:

> *Webster was much possessed by death*
> *And saw the skull beneath the skin;*
> *And breastless creatures underground*
> *Leaned backwards with a lipless grin.*

> *Daffodil bulbs instead of balls*
> *Stared from the sockets of the eyes!*
> *He knew that thought clings round dead limbs*
> *Tightening its lusts and luxuries.*

The first half of the poem is continued and concluded with the following verses:

> *Donne, I suppose, was such another*
> *Who found no substitute for sense,*
> *To seize and clutch and penetrate;*
> *Expert beyond experience,*

> *He knew the anguish of the marrow*
> *The ague of the skeleton;*
> *No contact possible to flesh*
> *Allayed the fever of the bone.*[1]

The 'fever of the bone'; the 'thoughts clinging round dead limbs' . . . These lines express the same fear, it seems, of an 'eternal, uneasy sensuality' which is the theme of THE INFERNO.

[1] Quoted from *Collected Poems* 1909–1935 by T. S. Eliot, Faber and Faber (first published 1936), p. 53.

IMAGINATIVE COMPOSITIONS

To return to the method of composition, the use of colour and other characteristics of the abstractions: many typical features are found in the SURRENDER OF BARCELONA (Pl. 16). We see another inverted T in the design, the crosspiece formed by the horizontal frieze of armoured figures at the base of the picture, the vertical stroke by the cylindrical tower placed nearly in the middle of the canvas, round which the whole composition is planned. Behind the tower the palaces, fortresses and two other symmetrically placed towers create innumerable vertical lines; and the strong downward thrust of all these buildings, as of so many shuttles or pistons, is checked by the horizontal frieze of figures. In the FOUR FIGURE COMPOSITION (Pl. 23) the vertical thrusts of the figures and the background panels are similarly arrested, at the base of the canvas, by the horizontal strip of light colour. Again, the earthy floor of the cave in the STATIONS OF THE DEAD (Pl. 19) forms the necessary horizontal contrast to the closely ranged, vertical figures.

The method of composition round a centrally placed block—like the tower in the SURRENDER OF BARCELONA and like the slightly inclined mechanical man in the PLAYERS ON THE STAGE (Pl. 20)—is repeated in the MUD CLINIC (Pl. 21) where a puce coloured, upright pedestal is placed almost exactly across the two axes of the picture. The colour itself is typical of the harsh, dissonant tones Wyndham Lewis so often deliberately introduced into the abstractions of the thirties. Again, in the CUBIST MUSEUM,[1] the horizontally placed light blue table also occupies an almost mathematically central position on the canvas. Both the pedestal in the MUD CLINIC and the table in the CUBIST MUSEUM catch the eye quickly by virtue of placing and brightness of colour. These centrally placed blocks give enormous stability to each of the four compositions in which they are found. The placing of a central block as a method of design is in a good sense an architectural procedure and the method will be discussed again in connection with the portraits.

The SURRENDER OF BARCELONA (Pl. 16) is a brightly coloured architectural fantasy, sunlit and unemotional. Warfare, siege and surrender appear to proceed according to established rules and the soldiers parade themselves in brisk, military order. At first the picture presents no overtones of sentiment, no sense of tragedy. But there is the detail of the hanged man which suddenly suggests that the whole picture is not, too readily, to be interpreted as a purely formal, brightly fantastic historical pageant. The note of tragedy is there, after all. We begin to make connections, remembering the Spanish Civil War of 1937. . . . The hanged man is easily overlooked—the figure is suspended from a large block standing before the base of the central tower—but once seen it is the kind of incidental touch that heightens the drama of a picture, deepening and sometimes changing its significance. The hanged man is typical of the apt but disquieting surprises Wyndham Lewis often introduces into the abstrac-

[1] Exhibited R.G.R.E., No. 114.

63

tions. Another example occurs in the STATIONS OF THE DEAD. In the queue of resigned figures, waiting, it seems, to be summoned through the door, we suddenly realize that one of them is not, like the others, standing on the ground, but that it is floating in the air, uncompromisingly in a state of levitation. And in a very different kind of picture, where the PLAYERS ON THE STAGE (Pl. 20) present themselves like masked sandwich men, bombastic or cringing, and freshly painted as if for a new season, we ultimately find that the mood of the picture is less straightforwardly satirical or pantomimic than was at first to be surmised. For among the reflections of the four figures we discover a fifth figure which has no business to be there. If the figures were to look down into the reflection they would not be able to account for the fifth image. It would be, for them, like the experience of the mountaineers who sensed the presence of an additional member of their party. 'Who is it?' they would ask, '. . . who is that on the other side of you?' In this case the situation gains piquancy because the onlooker sees the reflection and the figures in the picture do not. Finally, a disquieting mood is introduced into a picture by slight formal means in the INCA WITH BIRDS (Pl. 22). It is true that the birds are mentioned in the title, but they are very lightly drawn and painted, they are well in the background, and they are dwarfed by the Inca on the left. Yet their significance is out of all proportion to their weight and treatment. For with their oddly knowing expression, and unfledged heads, all beaks and eyes, they become the most important characters in the picture. They are entirely responsible for the disquieting and dreamlike air pervading the whole scene. Without the birds the picture would be a formal study in abstraction like the BLACK AND RED PRINCIPLE, for example. But as a result of the birds the picture stirs the imagination, haunts the memory.

The significance of these and similar details can of course be over-emphasized, their meaning over-interpreted. But they are typical of the unexpected devices, of a literary nature, abounding in the abstractions. They are partly responsible for the expanding afterthoughts arising out of Wyndham Lewis's work, inviting speculation outside the context, beyond the limits suggested by formal means. Remembering the INFERNO, the GROUP OF SUPPLICANTS, the visionary nature of pictures like the SURRENDER OF BARCELONA and ARMADA, and in view also of the details just discussed, Wyndham Lewis may, in a good sense, be called a painter of ideas. This is to suggest that many of his pictures are in a rare category, for the expression of ideas on canvas would seem to be left almost exclusively to the expressionists and surrealists, and Wyndham Lewis is not one of them.

There is, finally, one other picture which demands special attention within the category of the mixed idiom, yet it is not an abstraction in the same sense as the previous examples. THE CONVALESCENT (Colour Plate C) is not a visionary, satirical or literary picture; it does not invite questions as to its meaning; and the figures are simplified in a manner so straightforward that they could not be symbols of anything except themselves. This picture is an example of 'pure' painting, and it may be described as lyrical.

Here, as in the PORTRAIT OF EZRA POUND (Pl. 47) and in BEACH BABIES (Pl. 13), the figures are arranged diagonally. A very important feature of the design in BEACH BABIES is the wedge-shaped block aimed, so to speak, at the 'Babies' ' heads; and the composition of the CONVALESCENT is built up in numerous similarly tapered shapes. The two figures are arranged across a large and easily discerned block, like a truncated cone, running from base to upper edge of the canvas. The angles of the cone are governed at the top by the angles at the ends of the blind slats. The semi-reclining figure forms a diagonal across this cone and is supported from below by a firm, vertical block. The figure is weighted down across the thighs by the head of the companion-consoler. The danger of a see-saw movement—a tendency for the head and shoulders to drop down and the feet to fly up into the air—is prevented by inclined lines running up towards the head (the lines forming the right-hand edge of the cone); and several tapered and inclined blocks are also arranged to press towards the head and shoulders at the upper right-hand corner of the canvas. On the left of the canvas, outside the cone shape, a vertical line drops down towards the knees, as it were pressing upon them. (This line fulfils exactly the same function as the vertical line running down towards the wrist in the PORTRAIT OF EZRA POUND, Pl. 47). And pressure is added at the extremity of the figure, again to prevent the see-saw movement, by the corner of the scarlet shape impinging on the shin bones. The feet—characteristically suppressed—are anchored in the bowl.

In terms of balance and counterbalance, of thrust and support, the mechanics of the picture may thus be described. In a picture showing at first glance a more than usually varied and even apparently haphazard arrangement of lines and shapes, with comparatively few verticals and horizontals to ensure equilibrium, stability and poise are still seen to depend upon a carefully calculated structure. To those who are impatient of this kind of analysis—who believe, it may be, that an artist achieves his results not by calculation but by 'feeling'—it may be said that in the trained artist calculation and feeling about precision of balance, for example, are the same thing. The artist blocks in a figure at an angle, let us say; he 'feels' that some support is needed beneath the head, to prevent the impression that the figure may slip: and some lines are put in to prevent this possibility. Whether it be called feeling or calculation, the lines go in, though of course the artist may not rationalize the process while he is painting. And perhaps it is worth adding that here, at any rate, an analysis is worked out in terms of feelings, even if it is later expressed in an impersonal manner.

This is to discuss the picture from the point of view of construction, two dimensionally. Now the left-hand edge of the cone is made up of a line starting in the lower left-hand corner where it is formed by the shins of the reclining figure. This line is continued by the angles at the left-hand edge of the blind slats. As a *construction* line it is seen in one plane, two-dimensionally. But of course this line is broken by implied dimension: the shins are in the foreground, the blinds are in the background. The artist who creates the impression of space —the illusion of the third dimension—must always plan the picture so that it works well in two ways at once: as a flat design and as a well-filled space. This is particularly important as the two planes are, as it were, so close to each other, in reality in one plane, so that both the flat design and the created space effects are perceived at a glance, without a change of focus of the eyes. In the case of the CONVALESCENT it is notable that the illusion of space is achieved entirely by juxtaposition of tone and colour, certain tones advancing, others receding, and without recourse to perspective lines. (Though perhaps association also helps: inside a room we are accustomed to seeing a window *behind* a group of figures.) But colour is all-important; indeed the use of colour in this picture probably places it among the finest canvases the artist has ever produced.

A glow radiates from the picture and it is possible to bask in its warmth. There are various passages of peacock blue and green, and several strips of black, but warm tones predominate. The glow is set up by the triangle of tomato-scarlet in the lower left-hand corner; the reclining figure is picked out in rich, luminous yellows; and the head of the companion is painted in hot, light browns and reds. Charming local tones appear all over the canvas, sustaining an interest in colour at the near view. Below the tea-tray, on the pedestal, there are neutral shades in mushroom colours; and to the right of this pedestal an apricot tone appears. The feet of the reclining figure disappear into the bowl painted in yellow ochre. All these hot browns and yellows, pinks and scarlets, are emphasized by the rich Van Dyck brown of the slats across the window, and by the deep bottle-green shape behind the head of the reclining figure. The slats are arranged to drive the eye towards the head and their velvet texture seems both to obstruct and absorb the light from without; their darkness increases the radiance of the light within. There is a particular, an almost palpable atmosphere inside a shuttered room when the light outside is seen and felt only indirectly. In the CONVALESCENT Wyndham Lewis has captured this atmosphere and he has done so by the most delicate and sensitive use of colour; reds softly blooming, yellows gently resonant. It is, I believe, the only picture in which he has attempted to convey an atmosphere of this kind, and it is a masterpiece.

2

Portraits and Drawings from Life

Like the abstractions in the mixed idiom, portraits and drawings from life (other than the very early examples from student days) first appeared after the 1914–18 war. There are no sharp changes of style in this category—as between the Vorticist 'Plan' drawings, for example, and the post-Vorticist abstractions—though many groups of work may be identified by typical features. These groups are selected for discussion.

Life drawing may be used by the artist as a discipline: for the discovery of facts, or as an opportunity for the development of style. After the war, Wyndham Lewis was already a mature artist with considerable achievements behind him. The life drawings of 1919, typified by strong washes in red-brown, blue and green, reveal an interesting combination of discoveries and impositions (see RED NUDE, Pl. 27)[1]. They convey that sense of shock which follows when an artist sees something (and makes us see it) as if for the first time; yet there are also signs of the mature mind asserting its view of reality, selecting features according to the habits and requirements of a formed style. Swiftly and evenly laid, incisive lines trace the contours, always of a female nude, in a series of sweeping convexities. (A line is concave or convex according to the area it defines. In these drawings Wyndham Lewis emphasizes the outward, rounded curves of the body.) To follow the lines down the body of a standing nude, or round a squatting figure, is almost to feel the bite of pencil on paper, the swinging rhythms of free draughtsmanship controlled, as in the abstractions, not merely by the fingers but by the whole arm. But whereas, in the life drawings, there is the same confident spontaneity and evident pleasure in draughtsmanship already noted in the abstractions, there is also a personal and vital quality in the line arising, no doubt, out of the nature of the work. There will be more to say, later, about the formal characteristics of the line in the life drawings. Meanwhile one fact is important: in the abstractions, the very large majority of the

---

[1] Besides the drawing here reproduced other examples of washed life-drawings may be seen in the Ovid Press Folio, *Fifteen Drawings: the Nudes*, Nos. 1, 2, 3 and 4. Six other drawings in the folio date from this year.

drawings were made in ink; whereas in the life work the medium (with important exceptions)[1] is usually pencil or crayon. In 1919 the latter medium was the favourite. The drawings show no trace of scaffolding, most of them were probably made in ten minutes and painted as quickly. The dark washes were nevertheless added with great skill to give cohesion to the whole figure. Particular care was given to the areas of reflected light, also to that fascinating shadow lying between these areas and passages lit by the actual source. If in these drawings the contour curves are to some degree imposed, the washes are usually laid with regard for visual truth. They impart a remarkable sheen to the flesh.

It is a commonplace to remark on the frequent use by artists of favourite studio properties—certain tables and chairs, for example, a brass ornament, or a blouse. Whether these properties stimulate a particular kind of result, or whether the property is chosen because it suits a mood or picture, it would usually be difficult to say. But the use of properties is often confined to a group of paintings or drawings from a given period and the appearance of a particular chair, for example, may be a guide in the absence of dates. In the life drawings of 1920 and 1921 new characteristics of treatment are accompanied by the repeated use of certain properties. A Windsor chair, for instance, appears in many of the drawings (see GIRL IN A WINDSOR CHAIR, Pl. 28, also Mr Newton's description, p. 22), though in the example reproduced the legs of the chair do not receive detailed attention, the emphasis being on the figure. In the WOMAN IN A RED TAM O' SHANTER[2] the chair is represented very faithfully and this drawing, as it happens, shows all the properties of the period. The figure sits at a card table (another property), wearing a long frock with stripes at hem and cuffs. The same frock appears in several other drawings and in the oil-painting PRAXITELLA of 1921 (Temple Newsam House, Leeds). The tam o' shanter itself and the sleeveless jacket with its link buttons also occur in numerous drawings. Finally, there are the heavy eyebrows—the most common of all the characteristics of the period—often filled in with black paint or left in the form of two open lines as in the GIRL IN A WINDSOR CHAIR.

The linear style apparent in the drawings remains more or less constant throughout the work in the years to come; though naturally there are variations and developments. By degrees the colour is further subdued until it becomes, when employed, the faintest buff or yellow wash. The life drawings of the early 'twenties are superseded by the portrait drawings of the 'thirties; and these in turn are followed by the studies for the portraits in oil. But the essentials remain the same; and indeed the syntax of the life drawings, the nature of the line, is the key factor in Wyndham Lewis's style as a draughtsman.

To illustrate this essential characteristic of style, the nature of the line, the following examples may be quoted: the STUDY OF AN ELDERLY MAN, 1920

---

[1] See, for example, NUDE ON A COUCH (Editor's title), reproduced in *The Pavilion*, p. 6.

[2] Exhibited R.G.R.E., No. 1, reproduced in the Catalogue. Note p. 94.

(Pl. 30); the portrait drawing of MRS DESMOND HARMSWORTH, 1932 (Pl. 34); the WOMAN IN AN ARMCHAIR, 1936 (Pl. 38); and the sketch of EZRA POUND, 1938 (Pl. 46). These and countless other drawings show superb portraiture, startling virtuosity—not here the 'careful cultivation of a moderate talent' —and an emphatically masculine vigour and intensity. And they show that the line is geometric, architectural: architectural not only in the sense that it is clean and precise, intolerant of soft evasions, drawn as though for a blue-print; but architectural also in the shapes it assumes and suggests. The emphasis is still on the convex curves but they are answered and balanced by appropriate concavities. And it is particularly in the juxtaposition of curves, it seems to me, that this essential, and most easily recognized, characteristic of style is to be seen. It is as though Wyndham Lewis had discovered in the skulls and skeletons, in the flesh and in the clothes of human beings, the geometries of a classical order, the fluid line of Gothic tracery, the indefinable curves and angles of a modern architectural plan. He has described the process—more perfectly, perhaps, than he realized—as '. . . *burying Euclid deep in the living flesh*'.[1] This phrase, it will at once be understood, lends validity to the comparisons with geometry; and Euclidean geometry is the basis of many features in the design and construction of classical architecture. A perfect example of architectural-geometric curves, concave flowing into convex (in this case showing the traditional narrow strip or fillet at right-angles between them), may be seen very clearly in the eyebrow lines and forehead shadows of THE WOMAN IN AN ARMCHAIR, already quoted. This detail precisely resembles an architect's section of a moulding. But throughout the drawings we repeatedly find, here in the corrugations of a sleeve, there at the base of a skirt, in the shadows round the eyes, in the interlocking fingers—contexts are too numerous to quote specifically—the curves of a cornice, of a toros moulding, cyma recta, cyma reversa, ovola and the rest. The lines are incised with finality, intended to endure like an entablature carved in granite.

The display of whorls and voutes and Gothic apices in the drawings of Wyndham Lewis might lead one to expect a number of strict architectural studies. Only one exists. (I am excluding here the architectural fantasies noted in the abstractions, and the incidental architectural details later to be mentioned in connection with the portraits.) This drawing,[2] dated 1922, was made in Venice as a demonstration for Captain Guy Wyndham. The treatment emphasizes the verticality of a Gothic palace and campanile. This example excepted, a careful search does not reveal more than a very few scraps of strict architectural detail in the whole range of accessible work. There is the fluted column with one Ionic volute in the PILLAR of 1927, Pl. 6; a column appears in the

---

[1] *Wyndham Lewis the Artist*, p. 59, Editor's italics.

[2] VENETIAN PALACE (Editor's title). Present owners: the Mayor Gallery. The drawing is mentioned in *Blasting and Bombardiering*, pp. 236 and 237.

drawing ATHANATON of 1933, Pl. 10; and the base of a cornice moulding is seen in the upper left-hand corner of the portrait of EZRA POUND, Pl. 47. But that is all. Again, the artist's style might lead one to anticipate strict studies of musical instruments. None exist. (There is a kind of mandolin, not treated with great deliberation, on the pedestal in the TANK IN THE CLINIC.) The involutions at the head of a fiddle, like the mouldings of a cornice, are, as it were, ready-made Lewis shapes: and we might imagine that for this artist a stringed instrument would form a perfect subject. As Mr Newton has suggested, the fact is that Wyndham Lewis sees the fiddles, with their lovely curves, in the draperies of a human figure. There, too, he sees all that he requires of architecture, and he makes his own human 'order'.

The portrait drawings made in the years immediately following 1921 do not display any characteristics not so far discussed. The later years of the 'twenties —the *Enemy* period—were largely devoted, as we have seen, to abstractions in pen and ink. The next group of portrait drawings was made in 1932, the well-known 'THIRTY PERSONALITIES' exhibited in that year and published at the same time in folio form. The whole astonishing collection, pencil drawings of celebrated public figures, was made in two months. On the subject of portrait drawings the artist has said: 'To get a likeness must be our constant endeavour.'[1] One of the drawings in this series caused Sickert to exclaim that Wyndham Lewis was the 'greatest portraitist of this, or any other, time'. The drawing of MRS DESMOND HARMSWORTH (Pl. 34) is probably one of the finest examples.

With the THIRTY PERSONALITIES we approach the period dominated by the oil-paintings, both portraits and abstractions. Isolated examples of portraits have appeared in previous years, notably the PORTRAIT OF THE ARTIST of 1921 (Frontispiece), but during the 'thirties, and abroad, during the last war, a long series in this genre compels special attention. There is a notion, recently very prevalent, and not yet quite dead, that portrait painting is an 'impure' art form: the idea being that in portraiture the artist prostitutes his integrity, his style, his genius (or whatever it may be called) in the services of imposed, external requirements with which he should not be concerned. I believe this attitude to belong to the period, now passing, when all kinds of desperate arguments were needed to extol abstraction. But arguments which recommend abstraction at the *expense* of realism are now, happily, growing obsolete. We are even becoming accustomed, without talk of prostitution or impurity, to the fact that abstraction and realism, including even portraiture, may be practised by one and the same artist. Indeed, this increasingly common dual capacity, far from being decried, is to be anticipated almost as a matter of course. But this enlightenment did not obtain when in England, thirty years ago, Wyndham Lewis was the first to produce both forms of art at the same time. As a result, his reputation as an artist has suffered, on and off, ever since. He got the worst

---

[1] *Blasting and Bombardiering*, p. 68.

of both worlds. His portraits could not at first be credited because he also produced abstractions; and later his abstractions were regarded with suspicion because he also produced portraits. Fortunately it is now possible to judge both kinds of work on their own merits.

At an exhibition of miscellaneous works, by one artist or by several artists, it is usually possible to walk round the gallery making, at will, the adjustments required by landscape or portrait, still life or abstract, according to the type of picture on the wall ahead. A technique is in play, varying with the individual, which is customarily summoned at an exhibition of paintings. But at the recent Retrospective Exhibition of Wyndham Lewis's work (see Chronological Outline, p. 47)—where eight of his portraits were hanging in competition, as it were, with other examples of his own very forceful pictures—technique was of no avail. These life-size portraits were arresting, of course, in a sense that was to be anticipated, but they were also responsible for a disquieting impression that was not immediately comprehensible. Commanding attention, they did not readily permit one to pass on; for they made an almost embarassingly *personal* impression. It was to an unexampled degree like being under observation. And if, after a time, the shock wore off, it was not because the portraits lost their power but because one became reconciled to a series of personal encounters. And perhaps the most distinctive feature of Wyndham Lewis's portraits is this startlingly vivid, alive, *actual* quality—a feature quite unrelated, of course, to the matter of likeness. The intensity he bestows seems to transform a portrait into a presence.

And yet, paradoxically it might seem, the presence or personality of these portraits is distant and remote. They do not show the characteristics of romantic works, where the subjects radiate a warm, human appeal, inviting your acquaintance, your emotional interest in their affairs. The portraits have, rather, a classical, or a neo-classical air—like the work of Ingres—where the subject, having gained attention, remains entirely self-sufficient, as it were indifferent to the advances of a spectator. Religious connotations aside, each portrait might have as its sub-title '*Noli Me Tangere*'.

The achievement of a likeness in the portraits is never called in question. Yet despite full attention to expression, to intimate details of clothing, to what one accepts as a characteristic pose, we are conscious of the bones beneath the flesh, particularly in the heads and in the hands. The unseen skeleton always plays its important part. A similar care over underlying construction is important to the composition of each picture seen as a whole. Wyndham Lewis is not interested in the impressionistic sketch, the casual arrangement of his material. In keeping with his desire for a work that endures, that is fit to endure as a permanent record of his subject, his portraits are composed with almost the same rigorous formality as the abstractions in the mixed idiom: we see the same strong vertical and horizontal lines and a similar rectangularity of construction.

But while planned and deliberate backgrounds lend enormous dignity to the sitters, it is one of Wyndham Lewis's remarkable achievements that the backgrounds are never over-emphasized. As usual, every part of the canvas is strictly disciplined. Yet in nearly all the portraits there are incidental passages of great beauty and interest. And it is with reference to the incidentals and accessories that the composition of the portraits must be discussed.

The use of vertical and horizontal lines may be seen in each of the examples reproduced. In the portrait of MISS EDITH SITWELL (Pl. 37), for example, vertical lines from the upper and lower edges of the canvas meet a series of horizontals which drive the eye towards the seated figure. The figure, which is the focus of a whole system of rectangles, receives thrusts from all sides and absorbs them within itself. In the portrait of MRS NAOMI MITCHISON (Pl. 43) the nearly vertical line of the forearm, between chin and book, is echoed by vertical lines on either side of the figure. The horizontal movement set up by the book, zigzagging across the canvas, is emphasized by four horizontal lines near the top of the picture. And in the portrait of EZRA POUND (Pl. 47) the diagonal movement set up by the lines of the figure (and echoed by the edges of the newspaper and the sweep of the table edge) is securely stabilized by vertical lines at the left-hand edge of the canvas. The edge of the table support, continuing the lines of the canvas-within-the-picture, meet the hand at exactly the right point to give stability to the whole arrangement. Without these vertical lines the figure would appear to be over-weighted by the head, and might tend to slip down in the canvas. (Similar construction lines in THE CONVALESCENT will be recalled.)

The RED PORTRAIT (Pl. 41) may be taken as a final example among many others. Here it is necessary to mention at once the very unusual position of the model in a picture of this shape. The head is placed at exactly half its height above the horizontal centre line and the figure thus occupies the lower half of the canvas. This arrangement invites disaster: for the figure is in danger of appearing to fall out of the picture. Stability is assured by careful placing of particularly powerful vertical and horizontal lines, also by a very interesting rhythm running across the rectangles they form. Starting from the fire in the lower right-hand corner, the lines of the lap and the left arm lead the eye from hand to hand and up the standard of the lamp. From the shade of the lamp the eye crosses to the vase on the mantelpiece and is finally arrested by the dull red moon floating near it. This line, from fire to moon, is roughly elliptical in shape, travelling round the head; and it is this encircling motion which, besides increasing the poise and dignity of the figure, triumphantly perfects the composition. Apart from its lyric beauty this picture is a wonderful demonstration of success where the chances of success were reduced to a minimum at the outset.

Like many other examples, the RED PORTRAIT includes passages of abstraction.

The mirror above the fire-place reflects or reveals a landscape dominated by the red moon already mentioned. This scene helps to set the mood of the picture. The rapt and tranquil gaze of the sitter suggests that she is looking into a similar visionary landscape; and her pale face, materializing from the background like sculpture in high-light, might be lit by another moon. In the portraits of T. S. ELIOT (1938) Pl. 40, and MRS T. J. HONEYMAN (Pl. 36), there are areas of brilliantly coloured pattern with the shapes of flames and wings, birds and foliage, the kind of detail one associates with the abstractions in the mixed idiom. And, to quote three more examples, the sternly realistic portraits of JOHN MACLEOD (Pl. 48), MRS MITCHISON (Pl. 43), and STEPHEN SPENDER (Pl. 42), are each relieved by a series of pictures-within-pictures. Behind Mr John MacLeod there is a very interesting architectural fantasy of walls and towers, treated like the buildings in the SURRENDER OF BARCELONA (Pl. 16). Mrs Mitchison is accompanied by a sketch for a crucifixion. And Mr Spender's head partially covers one of two fragments of abstraction on the wall behind him. All these passages stand out very clearly, like the properties and features in these portraits—two particular chairs, for example, a waving line pattern on the fabric, the frequent use of a full-sleeved blouse—and further specific quotation is not required. On the subject of accessories in portraiture Mr Wyndham Lewis has said that they involve special problems and that he takes particular care over them. I imagine that the two abstract details in the portrait of Mr Spender would illustrate this point. Both are painted to suggest that the designs are continued, one behind the head, the other out of the picture. They are fragments, but fragments of a whole, and it looks as though the artist were copying examples of his own work. Yet both were, in fact, 'designed' for the portrait.[1]

It is care over the weight and placing of every detail in a portrait that ultimately ensures perfection of composition. But it is sometimes hard to appreciate niceties of placing when under the full impact of an original work. With sixty or seventy reproductions spread out on a table, and with the pictures reduced in size so that each one may be scanned at a glance, excellence or carelessness of placing stands out very sharply. (It is of course well known that a design is more readily perfected at a small size, when only a single pencil stroke or touch of colour need be added to rectify the balance or harmonize a tone. That is why artists so frequently square up their pictures from small sketches.) Reduced to the size of a reproduction the perfection of placing in the work of Wyndham Lewis is at once apparent. Yet he rarely employs the method of squaring up; and as with the life drawings, scaffolding of any kind is entirely absent. (Though

[1] The subject of accessories came up in conversation between Mr Wyndham Lewis and the Editor. The artist was at that time painting the sheaf of typescripts on the table beside Mr T. S. Eliot in the 'second' portrait (see Pl. B, note p. 82). It was on this occasion that Mr Lewis referred to the abstractions behind Mr Spender, confirming that these details had been invented for the picture.

the portraits are usually preceded by numerous preparatory sketches.) But the care over the placing, the rectangularity of design, and the formality of each canvas, may be quoted in evidence of that architectural approach to the painting, even of portraits, I have already mentioned. It is as if each canvas had been hoisted on to a drawing table and designed as minutely as the façade of a building.

But when, finally, we approach the question of colour, any suggestion of an architectural method is entirely out of place. It is well known that architects find it difficult to introduce colour into their work; and in the end they often despise it, talking (not without good reason, so far as architecture is concerned) of the 'dignity of monochrome'. For architecture is, fundamentally, an art dealing in line, rhythm and volume; and colour can rarely be used except as a flat *tone*. As Mr Newton has pointed out, the purity and dignity of some of Wyndham Lewis's drawings—those drawings, particularly, in which architectural features have been traced—would have been ruined by competitive effects of colour. But in the abstractions in oil, and here, in the portraits, colour becomes an integral part of the pictures. Colour helps to indicate the mood, it increases the impression of solidity and recession; and colour, patterned and contrasted, is so ingeniously woven into the whole composition that in many passages it would be difficult to tell which came first, the colour or the shape. In fact the two are often worked out together. Keen and powerful, at times wonderfully clear and brilliant, and occasionally employed, as we have seen, to provide a violent accent of disharmony, Wyndham Lewis's colour is above all as distinctly individual as his line.

Adopting chronological order, the SELF-PORTRAIT (Frontispiece) of 1921 is the first example for discussion. Power and delicacy combine in a result which perfectly evades potential faults. The portrait strikes hard, yet it is neither coarse nor over-simplified. The unique pale scarlet of the background, subdued by a milky diluent, is neither garish nor merely pretty. This background reveals traces of trial and error but it has been coaxed into beautiful harmony with the chocolate browns of the coat and hat. Other colours, making up a scheme of unusual combinations, appear in the mauve clock, outlined with blue, in the dark green of the canvas and in the unusual blue-green of the shirt. That harmony is maintained throughout is partly due to the neutralizing effect of the slab of white on the fire-place, between the sleeve and the canvas, and an adjacent strip of plain black.

It is always possible to analyse a picture according to different methods. Here it has been convenient to discuss first the construction of several examples, then the colour. Thus I have attempted to show that in the portrait of MISS EDITH SITWELL (Pl. 37), begun in 1923 and finished in 1935, the lines and shapes are strictly organized to direct the eye towards the figure. But the effect of the linear construction is subordinate to the effect of the colour. The passages of yellow in the skirt and green in the jacket—like fragments of broken glass—catch the eye at once. The greens and yellows are divided and intensified by a horizontal arrangement across the lap of small patches of very bright colour. Brilliantly vivid, these flickering notes of blue, red and yellow provide a centre of movement in a static work which might as a whole appear more harmonious without them; but without them it would be in danger of becoming over-exquisite, a too perfect equation. (To cover the scarf with a strip of paper, even in a reproduction, is to watch the picture lose all vitality.) The blues and browns surrounding the chair are seen to be echoes and combinations of the greens, reds and yellows previously noted. Soft greens, darker tones of leather-brown, are arranged to emphasize but not compete with the figure. The panels of bright blue in the background, though large in area, are a continuation of the blues of the scarf. The face alone is isolated from everything else in the picture: the delicate flesh tones are not repeated in any other passage. Even the hands —normally an important feature of the portraits—lie buried and invisible in the scarf on the lap. Their omission is another means of emphasizing the face; and their inclusion—given this pose—would have interfered with the vital contribution of the scarf. This picture shows everywhere signs of great care and thought and twelve years' intermittent work have wrought in it a wonderful unity. In terms of linear construction it is a perfect composition. It is also one of Wyndham Lewis's greatest portrait paintings, an architectural monument in colour.

In many of the portraits Wyndham Lewis allows one colour to dominate the whole canvas. The PORTRAIT OF MISS CLOSE,[1] for example, is painted largely in blue tones. The portraits of THE SMILING GENTLEMAN[2] and of JOHN MACLEOD (Pl. 48) are both typified by shades of grey, a grey sometimes deepening into blue, or turning into silver in the lighter areas. The second portrait of T. S. ELIOT (Pl. B) is another outstanding example in which blue dominates, but in this case the colour, though matt, is exceptionally dark and intense. Indeed the variety of blues in the canvases of Wyndham Lewis is particularly re-markable. Like steel, like passages from many different skies (though skies are never the background for a portrait: the sitters are invariably placed in a room), the blues are never the same. But powdered and silvery, light or dark, they have this in common: they are normally flat and cold. They belong to the English climate where the light is the light of the Gothic North.

But there are lyrical pictures in which an emotional warmth is conveyed by the use of reds and yellows. In LA SUERTE,[3] for example, the background area includes a familiar steel grey, and a kind of chestnut brown, both of which push forward and enrich the dusky saffron of the figure and table. And there are

[1] Exhibited R.G.R.E., No. 127.

[2] Exhibited R.G.R.E., No. 108.

[3] Tate Gallery, No. 5039. Formerly available reproduced at post-card size in colour.

also the portraits of the artist's wife, FROANNA[1] and the RED PORTRAIT (Pl. 41), both dominated by red-brown tones. With a basis, perhaps of Venetian red, Indian red, or madder brown, each picture shows innumerable varieties of tone, all radiating warmth. The fire in the RED PORTRAIT glows like a brazier, the moon in the abstract landscape is a dull red harvest moon. Here and there in each picture the basic colour is worked up into high-lights of gold, into uncompromising orange, into shades reminiscent of hot-coloured, hot-tasting tropical fruit. But even with the nearness of the fire in the RED PORTRAIT, and in spite of the drawn curtains in FROANNA, in neither case is the effect stifling or oppressive. Each picture is refreshed by passages of blue: a very cold blue above the fire in the RED PORTRAIT, another blue in the lamp standard; and an electric blue, in FROANNA, is arranged in streaks and rivulets on the dressing-gown like water held in the leaves of a plant. And, in both pictures, there are the pale flesh tones of face and hands for which the rich warmth of the backgrounds is the perfect setting.

Following these close-range observations on detail and style, perhaps in conclusion one or two general observations will not be out of place. It is noteworthy, for example, that Wyndham Lewis's work is never vulgar, never bourgeois, never parochial. The visits to France and Germany, Holland and Spain, when he was a student; and the visits to the Continent since then, and to Venice, the Barbary Coast, Canada and the U.S.A., have all left their mark. But the influence of travelling shows itself less in specific, iconographer's detail, or in the stamp of foreign schools, than in a certain breadth of character which can only be described as cosmopolitan. It is true, of course, that his portraits are the work of an Englishman working in England; and since nearly all his subjects are English men and women it would perhaps be a criticism if this were not the case. But the abstractions, it seems to me, might have been produced in Spain, France, Italy, Mexico, pre-Nazi Germany or America. Yet at the same time there is a passionate, an almost fanatically personal stamp in his work that lifts it away from the context of any one country, particularly, I think, from the context of England. There is a a sense in which his work may be said to lie outside nationality.

Related to the cosmopolitan character of his work is the difficulty of finding the appropriate pigeon-hole for it. For the term 'cubist' really will not do. This is not to deny certain Picasso-Braque cubist characteristics in the early work of over thirty years ago; but the abstractions since then are not cubist in at all the same sense. And Wyndham Lewis is not an expressionist; he is not a surrealist; and the terms 'classical' and 'romantic', as Mr Newton has pointed out, do not, without much qualification, assist us to place him. Unlike Picasso

---

[1] Glasgow Art Gallery. Reproduced in colour, *Picture Post*, March 1939, accompanying Dr John Rothenstein's article on Wyndham Lewis.

who may be put into almost any pigeon-hole (having labelled most of them himself), Wyndham Lewis finds a place in only one, and it is lettered with his own name.

I have described Wyndham Lewis's work as positive and masculine. The characteristics of his work that prompted that description are partly explained by the following passage from one of his own books: '. . . a method', he writes, 'which does not secure that definition and logical integrity that, as an artist, I require, I am, I admit, hostile to from the start. But no doubt what made me, to begin with, a painter, was some propensity for the exactly defined and also, fanatically it may be, the physical and the concrete'.[1] This statement is also the declaration of a man who never softens towards melancholy or nostalgia; he is not interested in the tattered physicalities of decay, however richly textured; and he refuses without compromise to identify himself with the decadence of his own time. Indeed he ignores equally the autumnal moods, the dripping grottos, the lakeside sedgerows which nowadays appeal so deeply— which are, for artists, a specific for success. Whether or not, historically speaking, we at the present time are at the end or at the beginning of an epoch is a well-known speculation; and we are not here concerned with the answer. But Wyndham Lewis eschews the backward glance; he looks forward, he is an innovator, he assists at the beginning of things. And his positive attitude, his temperamental incapacity to participate in the stream of decay, give further point to that description of himself as a 'Renaissance man'.[2]

And finally there is his self-confidence, his belief in himself—another Renaissance attribute—demonstrated by that lordly touch which gives to some of his pictures the authority of a philosophical utterance. Wyndham Lewis's work shows the confidence found in the work of all good artists, but it is accompanied by a certain humility of the spirit. I do not mean to suggest that Wyndham Lewis pretends to regard himself as an indifferent artist, or that he indulges in false modesty. (Parenthetically, it is a fact, very soon discovered in his company, that he is deeply critical of shortcomings in his own work.) By humility I mean something rather different. As the following passage will show, he acknowledges that he is, in a sense, a vehicle; that artistic creation involves co-operation between himself and some source of power access to which is the particular privilege of the artist. This passage, it seems to me, reveals

[1] *Time and Western Man*, p. 129.

[2] The description is well supported by his breadth of curiosity and versatility of talent. There is also the Renaissance preoccupation with figures and portraiture. This has always been so strong, so exclusive of other subject material (as the reproductions and notes in this book will have shown), that it is to be doubted whether Wyndham Lewis has ever made a sketch or painted a landscape 'from the life' since the days when he was a student; at any rate none appear to survive. But the non-participation in open-air painting is not due simply to his interest in figures. For one thing, open-air painting and the production of naturalist landscapes nearly always involve some kind of impressionism; and he has been working away from impressionist methods ever since 1912.

Wyndham Lewis in a very sympathetic light, and forms a fitting conclusion to this brief discussion of details in his work. Writing in 1927 he says: 'I will try to state very briefly my own belief as to the true character of artistic creation. The production of a work of art is, I believe, strictly the work of a visionary. Indeed this seems so evident that it scarcely needs pointing out. Shakespeare, writing his King Lear, was evidently in some sort of a trance; for the production of such a work an entranced condition seems as essential as it was for Blake when he conversed with the Man who Built the Pyramids. To create King Lear, or to believe that you have held communion with some historic personage—those are much the same thing. The traditional romantic name for a poet—namely, "dreamer"—accurately describes all creative artists. . . .' And he continues, 'If you say that creative art is a spell, a talisman, an incantation—that it is *magic*, in short, there, too, I believe you would be accurately describing it. That the artist uses and manipulates a supernatural power seems very likely.'[1] There may, of course, be two opinions about the 'manipulation of a supernatural power'. So much Wyndham Lewis would himself concede. What is important is that he should make, and believe in, such a statement.

[1] *Time and Western Man*, p. 198.

78

4

Notes on the Plates

Notes on the Plates

Throughout the following notes the first of the size-dimensions indicates the height of the picture along the left-hand edge; the second, the width of the picture along the top.

All references to left or right-hand side of a picture are made from the observer's point of view unless otherwise stated.

An asterisk (*) against the title of a picture indicates that it has never before been reproduced.

In the case of undated pictures the year of completion, given in brackets, has been confirmed by the artist.

In most cases where drawings have been measured in the mount, this indicates that the mount has been stuck down. The size of the sheet could not then be discovered.

Unless otherwise stated the drawings are on white paper.

'Present ownership' indicates possession of the work concerned at the time of inquiry; i.e. on different occasions between May 1949 and May 1950.

The reader is referred to p. 35 for the key to the abbreviations used throughout these notes.

Title Page. HEAD OF MERCURY*

> This head shares characteristics of style with the heads of the archaic figures (*Two Figures*, Pl. 1, note p. 81) and the heads of the Robots in the designs for *Timon of Athens* (see example Pl. 3, note p. 84). Impulsively drawn like the archaic figures, it also has the geometric angularity and sharpness of the Robot figures and the Vorticist drawings. The jagged bars of shading, and the emphasis on the high cheek-bones—and the general treatment of the face as though it were a mask—are all typical of the work of 1912 and 1913.
>
> *Pen and blue ink. Size:* $15\frac{9}{16} \times 11\frac{9}{16}$ *ins. Unsigned, undated* (1912 *or* 1913).
> Present owner : the Artist.

Frontispiece, Colour Plate A. SELF-PORTRAIT OF THE ARTIST*

> In this head and shoulders portrait the artist stands with his left side towards the observer showing a three-quarter view of the face. Painted largely with the use of a mirror, a corner of the canvas on which he works can be seen on the left side of the picture. In the background a fire-place, with a clock and the corner of a table or pedestal.
>
> Colours: Face and neck light brown, heavily shaded in dark brown; coat and hat in dark brown; shirt blue-green; the table olive green, the back of the canvas in a different dark green. The background in pale scarlet; the fire-place black and white; the clock mauve, with a white centre and blue outlines.
>
> *Oil on canvas. Size* 30×27 *ins. Signed* (*undated*) *lower right hand-corner: Wyndham Lewis* (1921).
> Present owners: Rutherston Collection, No. 318.

81   F

NOTES ON THE PLATES

Exhibited under the auspices of the Arts Council, in a 'Selection from the Rutherston Collection—Oil Paintings', at various towns from January 1947 to March 1948: No. 17 in the 'hand-list'; also R.G.R.E. No. 126.

This is the only existing self-portrait in oils. Of the very numerous self-portrait-drawings the following example, despite the difference in date, seems most closely to resemble the painting above:

SELF-PORTRAIT

In this drawing also the artist wears a hat, the brim drawn to reveal the forehead. Here, however, he wears spectacles, and the hair is shorter; but the light casts shadows on the left side of his face, as in the above example, and the searching gaze (usually seen in self-portraits) is also present. The face and collar are washed in brown.

Pen and blue-black ink and water-colour washes. Size $10\frac{3}{4} \times 8\frac{1}{2}$ ins., mounted. Signed and dated in ink, lower left-hand corner of the drawing, vertically: WL 1932.
Present owner: J. Paton Walker, Esq.
Exhibited: R.G.R.E., No. 53, reproduced in the catalogue; also at the 'Portrait of the Artist' Exhibition, St George's Gallery, June 1950, No. 41.

Colour Plate B. PORTRAIT OF T. S. ELIOT (1949) (opposite p. 16)

The sitter is in a small armchair, head inclined slightly forward, knees crossed, hands on lap. Body and chair are turned a little to the right. The viewpoint is close, the onlooker's eyes on a level with the head. As in the 'first' portrait (Pl. 40, note p. 97), a large white pocket handkerchief is prominently displayed. In the lower left-hand corner a round-topped table supports an open set of typescripts.
Colours: The face cold and chalky, touched with pink and green. The suit a very deep blue, matt, intense; the tie black. The background near-white with hints of green and yellow, with also a dull blue strip along the upper left-hand edge of the canvas. Table dark brown, typescript in cold, light blue. The upholstery of the chair painted in light blue, with red and blue checks. Lines in dark yellow indicate the watch chain.

Oil on canvas. Size $34 \times 21\frac{3}{4}$ ins. Signed and dated vertically, along right-hand edge of canvas: Wyndham Lewis 1949.
Present owners: The Master and Fellows of Magdalene College, Cambridge.
Reproduced: *Time*, vol. 53, May 30, 1949, p. 60 (also with a reproduction of the 1938 portrait, Pl. 40, note p. 97).
Exhibited: R.G.R.E., No. 125.

Preliminary sketches for the above include:

PORTRAIT STUDY OF T. S. ELIOT

In this drawing the sitter assumes a pose almost identical with that seen in the portrait. The emphasis is on the carefully modelled face. The hands, firmly drawn, lie easily in the lap. Heavy shading appears on the tie and waistcoat, also on parts of the jacket and trousers. This study does not include details of the chair, table or typescripts seen in the finished portrait.

Black conté crayon. Size $21\frac{1}{2} \times 12\frac{1}{2}$ in., mounted. Signed and dated in crayon, lower left-hand corner: Wyndham Lewis 1949.
Present owner: Eric J. N. Bramall, Esq.
Provenance: The Leicester Galleries.

NOTES ON THE PLATES

Colour Plate C. THE CONVALESCENT (opposite p. 34)

The shape of a truncated cone, around and within which the picture is constructed, is readily discerned reaching from base to upper edge of the canvas and rather to the left of the centre. Across this cone the figure of the convalescent reclines diagonally. Outside the cone several formal, tapered, wedge-shaped blocks support the design. The reclining figure is painted in rich yellows and is surrounded by passages in tomato-scarlet, oatmeal, apricot, light pinks and other warm or hot tones. Here and there are small areas of blue and green. The blind slats are painted in Van Dyck brown. *Oil on canvas: Size 24 × 30 ins. Signed and dated lower right-hand corner: Wyndham Lewis 1933.* (Actually completed 1936.)
Present owner: Sir Colin Anderson.
Exhibited: Leicester Galleries, Wyndham Lewis exhibition 1937, No. 41, as THE INVALID; also R.G.R.E. No. 112 (reproduced in the catalogue); also 'The Private Collector', Contemporary Art Society exhibition, Tate Gallery, 1950, No. 140.

Colour Plate D. DRAGON IN A CAGE* (opposite p. 50)

Imposed upon a subsequently enriched 'plan' background of the Vorticist period (see note below), the dragon is placed at a slight angle, inclining inwards, at the right-hand side of the picture. The cage, ribs and neck of the dragon are seen in one plane, like an X-ray photograph; and the smoke can be seen coiling among the ribs and streaming up the dragon's neck. The dragon resembles a stove, its neck the stove-pipe, and the intention and effect of the drawing are thus satirical.
Colours: The dragon's cage and ribs are painted in black and white, orange and pale pink. This group, occupying the right-hand side of the picture, is arranged against a dark green background touched, here and there, with ultramarine, pale green and another pink. The left-hand side of the picture is filled with bars of black, orange and pale yellow against various pale, neutral washes. In the upper left-hand corner the bubble-like details are painted in very bright leaf green with touches of a soft, dark green and light yellow.
Pencil, red chalk, pen and black ink and water-colour washes: gouache. Size: 18½ × 5/16 ins., mounted. (The actual sheet size is larger by approximately ¼ inch in both dimensions.) Signed and dated in pencil, lower left-hand corner: Wyndham Lewis 1950.
Present owner: the Artist.
This very interesting work was first blocked-out in broad outline shortly before the 1914–1918 war. Thus the angular 'plan' construction of the background, and some details of the dragon itself, show Vorticist characteristics. But most of the colour is recently applied: for example, all the globes, bubbles, puffs of smoke; also the large areas of background colour to the left of the picture, and many of the strips and bars near to, and accompanying, the dragon. For this reason the drawing, when signed, was dated 1950. Numerous construction lines—two sets of squaring-up frames, in pencil and red chalk—can be clearly seen, particularly in the lower half of the drawing. Evidence of squaring-up is seen in no other example reproduced in this book.

Plate 1. TWO FIGURES*

An upright, female figure stands in profile, facing left, slightly to the right of the vertical centre line. The torso of the second, lying figure, inclines towards the left, supported by rocks. Both figures are sculptural, rock-like, the skulls irregularly hacked away above the forehead. Harsh features, large eyes. A rocky landscape, suggesting the moon; pale, flickering light. Figures in mushroom pink and rich brown; elsewhere, greys and buffs. Impulsive technique, deeply scored lines.

NOTES ON THE PLATES

Pencil, pen and ink and water-colour washes: gouache. Size: 12¼×9½ ins. Signed (undated) in pencil, lower right-hand corner: Wyndham Lewis (1912). The signature was added recently (July 1950) at the request of the owner, and after the photograph was taken.

Present owner: Charles Handley-Read, Esq.

Provenance: The Redfern Gallery.

Numerous related drawings include:

TWO WOMEN

In this drawing the heads and shoulders of the figures resemble sculpture in rock: heavy, angular and stratified. Colours are grey, pink and brown.

Pencil, pen and ink and water-colour washes: gouache. Size: 19×24¾ ins. Colour of paper: the two figures, drawn on white paper, are cut out and stuck on a dark grey paper background. Signed and dated in ink, lower right-hand corner: Wyndham Lewis 1912.

Present owners: The Arts Council of Great Britain.

Provenance: The Redfern Gallery.

Exhibited: R.G.R.E. No. 12; also at the 'Exhibition of Contemporary British Art', No. 60, when the New Burlington Galleries were reopened in November 1949.

Besides TWO WOMEN, above, twelve other examples from the same year were exhibited at the R.G.R.E. See also THE CENTAURESS, Pl. 5, note p. 85, and MAN AND WOMAN. Pl. 2, note below.

Plate 2. MAN AND WOMAN*

The narrow strip of ground at the base of the picture is tilted diagonally to the left. A pile of rock-like shapes in the lower left-hand corner. The background is empty except for two or three irregular areas painted in dark washes. Against this background, slightly to the right of the picture, the male figure stands as though crucified, but without a cross. To the left, sitting on the rocks, the female figure holds her hands on her lap. Figures, foreground and background washes are all painted in varying degrees of hot, dark brown.

Pen and ink, crayon and water-colour washes: gouache. Size: 14×9¾ ins., mounted. Signed and dated in ink, right-hand side, above diagonal line terminating foreground: Wyndham Lewis 1912. (The signature and date, now to be seen in the original, were added after the nearly contemporary photograph was taken; also after mounting: which explains why the 'is' of 'Lewis' appears beneath 'Lew'.)

Present owners: The Mayor Gallery.

The impulsive technique; the figures with their heavy torsos, angular skulls and knotted limbs; the background shapes and the rocky foreground; and the use of earth colours relate this drawing in all particulars with TWO FIGURES, Pl. 1, note p. 83. The 'replacement' of the head of the figure on the left should be noted, also the extension of the sheet at the base.

Plate 3. A design for the publication TIMON OF ATHENS

A view into a scene of blocks and bars of masonry, all the angles and segments leading to a focus—the vortex—near the top left-hand corner. Numerous robot figures are incorporated into the design, diminishing rapidly in size and thus increasing the effect of recession. Sharp, clean lines, geometric curves. Cold blues and browns. Many areas left unpainted, giving the impression of glaring white light.

Pen and ink and water-colour washes. Untraced. From a photograph of the plate in the publication. Size: unknown. Probably about 16×10 ins. Unsigned, undated (1913 or 1914).

NOTES ON THE PLATES

Of one of the five large similar designs reproduced in the publication (note p. 37), the following details are available:

DESIGN FOR TIMON OF ATHENS

Pen and ink and washes of ink and water-colour. Size: 16⅜×10¾ ins., mounted. Unsigned, undated (1913 or 1914).
Present owner: Rex Nan Kivell, Esq.
Exhibited: R.G.R.E. No. 34.
None of the reproductions in the publication is numbered or dated; five are signed *WL*.

Plate 4. PLANNERS

In this totally abstract drawing the eye is led to the focus or vortex in the centre by powerful diagonal lines running in from all four sides. A system of strips and bars, making irregular, plan-like shapes, is concentrated in the lower half of the sheet. In the upper half, a heavy black strip zigzags in from the left-hand edge and terminates (above the focus of the picture) in a shape not unlike a head. This black shape dominates the whole design. Black and white play an important part in the colour scheme, to which various clear blues and browns are added.
Pencil, pen and black ink, conté crayon and water-colour washes. Size: 12⅛×14⅝ ins. Signed (undated) in ink, diagonally, upper right-hand corner: Wyndham Lewis (1913).
Present owners: The Mayor Gallery.
Exhibited: R.G.R.E. No. 17. Reproduced in the catalogue.

Plate 5. THE CENTAURESS *

Sharply drawn, and washed in neutral shades of grey, the primitive figure of the Centauress stands low down in the middle of the sheet against a 'plan' background which heralds Vorticism. The background painted in bright colours: pink, light green, various blues.
Pen and ink and water-colour washes. Size: 12¼×14⅜ ins. Signed and dated in ink, lower right-hand corner: Wyndham Lewis 1912.
Present owner: Charles Handley-Read, Esq.
Provenance: The Mayor Gallery.
Exhibited: R.G.R.E. No. 20.
Other drawings of Centauresses include:

CENTAURESS, No. 2.
In this drawing the head and torso of the Centauress are shown in profile, facing right. The flat skull, cut off above the forehead, the jagged body and heavy ink lines are all typical of the work of the period. Colours: dark and light green and grey.
Pencil, pen and ink and water-colour washes. Size: 12¼×9⅝ ins. Signed and dated in ink, upper right-hand corner: Wyndham Lewis 1912.
Present owners: The Mayor Gallery.
Exhibited: R.G.R.E. No. 22.
For further details of Vorticism and 'Plan' backgrounds, see p. 52.

Plate 6. THE PILLAR *

A fluted pillar with one volute of an Ionic capital stands on the left. Beside it, to the right, an abstracted vertical figure is made up of shapes like those of an aeroplane propeller. From this figure a band of design extends to the right where it ends in a group of three vertical units, all parallel to the pillar. A spiral whorl, lower right, echoes the curves of the volute. Geometric shapes predominate, several like knife-blades with rounded backs.

Size: unknown. Signed (undated) in ink, lower right-hand corner of the design, vertically: WL (1927). Untraced. From a photograph in the possession of the artist.

Plate 7. BIRD AND FIGURE*

The torso of a male figure is placed horizontally across the base of the design, the head and elongated neck stretched out at a declining angle. Behind the fallen figure a series of shapes form a pointed, pyramidal support culminating in a bird's head. This head also belongs to a group of reiterated shapes, the bird's body and wings, flying out at an angle from the vertical support.

Pen and ink. Size: unknown. Signed and dated, lower right-hand corner: Wyndham Lewis 1925. Untraced. From a photograph in the possession of the artist.

The horizontal figure in this drawing, also the group flying out at an angle, may be compared with the corresponding horizontal and flying figures in the following example (mentioned on p. 55):

FIGURES IN THE AIR

Pencil, pen and ink, and washes of ink and water-colour. Size: $11\frac{1}{2} \times 6\frac{1}{2}$ ins., mounted. Signed and dated in ink, lower right-hand corner, diagonally: WL (twice) 1927.

Present owner: Wyndham T. Vint, Esq.

Exhibited: R.G.R.E. No. 94, as ON THE ROOF.

Reproduced: *The Enemy*, No. 1, in colour, opposite p. 14.

The 'flying' figures in both examples recall the rotary movement of a 'governor' bearing raised by centrifugal force.

Plate 8. SENTINELS

Two severely formalized winged figures with egg-shaped heads (pointed sharply at the chin) stand at the base line of the drawing. Behind the figures, in the background, two screens or niches. At the top of the design, left-hand corner, the volute of an Ionic capital; also a beam, like an architrave, extending to the right. Apart from the volute, the beam, and the suggestion of niches, the figures are surrounded by very carefully shaded shapes, angular and sharply drawn, forming a flickering abstract design.

Pen and black ink. Size: $9\frac{5}{8} \times 5\frac{5}{8}$ ins. Unsigned, undated (1928).

Present owner: the Artist.

Reproduced: *The Enemy*, No. 3, opposite p. 84.

The reproduction enlarges the design to nearly four times its actual size.

Plate 9. BAGDAD: A PANEL*

The picture is seen to be made up of four vertical strips roughly equal in width, running from base to upper edge of the panel. The strip at the left-hand edge of the panel includes a dark, muddy-coloured green tree in an ochre tub. Above the tree, dark, abstracted shapes. The second strip from the left is very light in tone with pink, blue and green patches: the lower half resembles a cardboard model of a staircase, painted near-white. These architectural shapes are simplified as they rise and terminate in a pink-toned shape like the head of a shell. The upper end of this panel is extended across to the right, forming the top of the third strip from the left. This strip includes, high up, a large, light blue disc; below the disc, a totemic torso with a classical mask-head (see p. 58) poised above a cylindrical block. The fourth strip (adjacent to the right-hand edge of panel), is formed by another totemic figure, tall, and with a mask-head painted in varying shades of brown. All four strips are linked together by fragments of design moving horizontally; and all four fade away into dark blue at the top of the panel. This was the first large painting in oils among the abstractions in the mixed-idiom.

Oil on two large sheets of plywood, jointed to show three divisions across the horizontal centre line. Size: 72 ×31 ins. Unsigned, undated (1927).
Present owner: A. Zwemmer, Esq.
Exhibited: R.G.R.E. No. 122.

Plate 10. ATHANATON* (Immortality)

The detail is concentrated at the sides of the sheet. To the right a system of abstract and near abstract shapes includes a column and part of a totemic design, the latter broken in the middle and leaning over towards the left. The diagonal block thus formed provides a link between the two sides of the picture. The detail on left includes several small, severely formalized figures; also a pair of eyes forming part of a mask; and a horizontal band of lettering at the top which includes the title. Other links between the two sides of the picture are formed by a strong block of dark colour behind the inclined end of the totem pole; also the horizontal, serrated ink lines running in bands across the base of the drawing. The latter resemble the symbol for sea along the edge of land in a map.
Colours: Black, yellow and orange, concentrated around the edge of the picture. The black area below the inclined pole is grey in the centre.

Pen and ink with ink and water-colour washes: gouache. Size: 10 ×11⅜ ins., mounted. Signed and dated in pencil, lower right-hand corner, vertically: Wyndham Lewis 1933.
Present owner: Arthur Crossland, Esq.
Exhibited: R.G.R.E., No. 88.

Plate 11. DUST WRAPPER FOR *THE APES OF GOD*

The drawing on the front cover shows an ape holding a brush and a palette. This figure symbolizes the satirical nature of the whole book. The design is printed in bright orange and a pale yellow-pink with black lines. It is remarkable not only for the drawing of the ape but for the very successful way in which the lettering is made to conform to the artist's style.

Untraced. From a photograph of the dust wrapper on the first, limited edition of the book. Unsigned, undated (1929). (Bibliographical note, p. 42.)
Dust wrappers designed and/or lettered by the artist for his own publications are noted in the Chronological Outline.

Plate 12. MONKS*

In the upper third of the drawing three monks are arranged as though ascending a hidden staircase. They move from left to right, their bowed heads forming a diagonal line. Their severely formalized robes are painted in black, white and ochre. Behind the monks, and to the sides of this area of the drawing, two sharply drawn, rectangular blocks, painted in buff tones, form the chief contrast to the curved shapes of the figures. Below the monks, the lower two-thirds of the drawing is filled by a wide variety of shapes and colours. Across the top of this area a brown figure, stretched out at full length, lies horizontally. Supporting it, several large, irregular shapes, arranged more or less diagonally, are painted in white, dark and light blues, orange and very strong green. Imposed upon these shapes a group of smaller patterns, like part of a totem pole, provide a vertical support to the horizontal figure; and birds' heads, beaks, wings and animal forms are here easily recognized, painted in reds, light browns, orange and black. There are also several touches of discordant puce. The horizontal figure.

with its vertical support at the centre, shows once again the familiar T construction. *Pencil and pen and black ink with washes in water-colour and inks: gouache. Size:* $13\frac{1}{16} \times 8\frac{1}{16}$ *ins. Signed and dated in ink, lower left-hand corner: Wyndham Lewis 1934.*
Present owner: J. A. White, Esq.
Provenance: The Zwemmer Gallery.

Plate 13. BEACH BABIES*

The two figures, painted in light browns, sit back at an angle on a sandy shelf near the sea. Their bodies form a diagonal line across the canvas. A piece of drapery in strong green hangs between them. The chaperon sits bolt upright at a lower level. A near-white vertical panel, left, heavily painted, rises out of the sand behind the Babies, and a tapered wedge, upper right, is arranged horizontally, pointing at the Babies' heads. Most of the background is pale in tone, with yellows, blues and greens. Earth colours appear in the figures.
Oil on canvas. Size: 20×40 *ins. Signed and dated lower left-hand corner, vertically: Wyndham Lewis* 1933. (Actually completed in 1936.)
Present owners: The Redfern Gallery.
Exhibited: Leicester Galleries, Wyndham Lewis exhibition, 1937, No. 33. Also R.G.R.E., No. 188; also International Exhibition of Paintings, Carnegie Institute, October–December, 1950; reproduced in the Catalogue, Pl. 88.

Plate 14. BEACH SCENE*

From the open sea on the right a strip of shallow water flows diagonally across the picture. Beyond the water, centre and left, a semi-abstract scene with maritime buildings on a cliff top. In the foreground, a diagonal strip of sand with three large bathing tents across the lower right-hand corner. Two figures are drying themselves near the centre tent; a third figure near the left-hand edge of the picture stands with a ball in upraised hands. In the water, near the middle of the picture, a group of five figures playing seaside ball-games.
Colours: White paint on the tents, touches of yellow-brown on the sand, various bright colours—reds and greens—on the distant cliff scene. The water suggested by areas of blue drawn in with a pen.
Pen and blue and black ink with washes in water-colour and ink: gouache. Size: $12\frac{1}{4} \times 16\frac{3}{4}$ *ins. Unsigned, undated* (*c.* 1929). *Colour of paper: light grey.*
Present owners: John P. Harthan, Esq., and Charles Handley-Read, Esq.
Provenance: The Zwemmer Gallery.
Exhibited: The London Gallery, 'The Cubist Spirit in Its Time', March–May 1947, No. 56; also R.G.R.E., No. 59.
One of a series of ten or twelve paintings on the theme of sport made for the late Lord Inchcape when Viscount Glenapp.

Plate 15. ROMAN ACTORS

Three column-figures, not unlike totem poles, are ranged across the sheet, reaching from upper to lower edges. All the heads are like masks. The left-hand figure faces front, the arms and torso readily discerned. The central figure is double-headed, the lower of the two heads facing right, with the head and hair (low on the forehead) of a classical mask. The right-hand figure faces left. At the right of the sheet, a vertical panel, not a figure, with decorative infilling. Behind the figures, rect-angular shapes (one including a contour of geometric curves) form a close background. Dominant colours: Black, white, cerise, vermilion, yellow and various browns.
Pencil and pen and ink with washes in water-colour and inks: gouache. Size: $15 \times$

$21\frac{1}{8}$ ins. Colour of paper: light grey. Signed (undated) in ink, lower right-hand corner, vertically: Wyndham Lewis (1934).

Present owner: Mrs Stanley Resor, New York.

Provenance: The Zwemmer Gallery.

Reproduced: 'Fantastic Art: Dada: Surrealism', The Museum of Modern Art, New York, p. 215.

Plate 16. THE SURRENDER OF BARCELONA

The picture is dominated by the cylindrical tower placed nearly vertically in the middle of the canvas. Behind it, two square towers are symmetrically placed before numerous closely-grouped buildings in a variety of architectural styles. Top left, a glimpse of sea and sails. Around and between the three major towers, numerous small, military figures, some with horses, others with lances and shields. Immediately before the central tower, the figure of a hanged man is suspended from a large block like a gigantic tree stump. Across the base of the picture a frieze of armoured figures. (Cf. the armoured figures in ARMADA, Pl. 17, note below.)

Colours: The buildings in various shades of yellow and brown; the sandy ground in lighter tones of yellow; the foreground figures in steely blue-greens. Accents of puce, very bright yellow and crimson in the pennants and roofs.

Oil on canvas. Size: $33 \times 23\frac{3}{8}$ ins. Unsigned, undated (1936).

Present owners: The Tate Gallery, No. 5768. Purchased out of the Knapping Fund.

Exhibited: Leicester Galleries, Wyndham Lewis exhibition, 1937, No. 38. as THE SIEGE OF BARCELONA.

Reproduced: Wyndham Lewis the Artist: from Blast to Burlington House, opposite p. 224, in colour; also Picture Post, March 1939, in colour, illustrating an article by Dr John Rothenstein (No. 26 in the series 'Great British Artists'); also The Studio, vol. 128, p. 185; also Pavilion, edited by Myfanwy Evans, I.T. Publications (N-D.), p. 5, in colour, illustrating an essay 'Towards an Earth Culture or the Electric Culture of the Transition' by the artist,

For further details of this picture, see p. 63.

Plate 17. THE ARMADA

Four large figures are ranged across the canvas in the foreground, presumably on the high deck of a galleon. The head of a fifth figure, at a lower level, fills the lower left-hand corner of the picture. Only one figure, perhaps a monk, is without armour. We see the side view of his face and the top of his habit. Ascetic, hermit-like, he might be an important religious, a kind of Father Joseph, at present under suspicion: he seems to be guarded like a prisoner. The armoured figures hold truncheons and shields, the right-hand figure with arm outstretched in command, the left-hand figure posed as though in a ballet. His face is an armour mask, part visor, part living flesh. On the water in the background, several galleons are at anchor, painted in very light, bright colours—yellows, orange, red. The sea is white, with a green tone added. The foreground figures show up strongly against the light background, the armour in dark steely-grey. The deck of the boat is painted in yellow merging to pink.

Oil on canvas. Size: 36×28 ins. Signed and dated, lower right-hand corner: Wyndham Lewis 1937.

Present owners: Vancouver Art Gallery, Canada.

Reproduced: Cahiers d'Art, vol. 13, Nos. 1–2, 1938, p. 33; The Listener, cover, May 1949.

Provenance: The Lefevre Gallery.

Exhibited: R.G.R.E., No. 25; also Vancouver, May 1951, in an exhibition 'Contemporary British Art' organized by the British Council. The exhibition was also scheduled to visit the following towns during 1951: Seattle, San José, San Francisco, Salt Lake City, Portland (Oregon).

Plate 18. DEPARTURE OF A PRINCESS FROM CHAOS*

The Princess stands in heavy drapery, light in tone, slightly to left of vertical centre line. Her head, tilted left, is heavily cowled. With her left hand she holds the drapery away from her face. She looks directly at the observer and appears to be in a somnambulistic trance. A frowning figure to the left, and two figures to the right, assist her departure. One of them holds a pigeon. The heads of the attendant figures are characteristic of the fantasy-abstractions (in the mixed idiom) of the thirties. The figures in the foreground are partially obscured by wisps of mist floating across them. In the background, left, a vision of figures in turmoil recalls the groups in the INFERNO; to the right, through a gap in a crumbling wall, a stormy sea with a boat and a bird, the latter in flight.

Few details of this picture are available as it has been over-painted since it was exhibited at the Leicester Galleries, Wyndham Lewis exhibition, 1937 (the year of its completion), No. 44.

In the catalogue Foreword to the exhibition the artist said of this picture: '. . . the DEPARTURE OF A PRINCESS FROM CHAOS is the outcome of a dream. I dreamed that a Princess, whose particularly graceful person is often present in the pages of our newspapers, was moving through a misty scene, apparently about to depart from it, and with her were three figures, one of which was releasing a pigeon. This dream, with differences, was repeated, and it was so vivid that, having it in my mind's eye as plainly as if it were present to me, I painted it.' The artist continues: 'As to the resemblance of the figure in the canvas to the Princess in question—whose face you all know well, and whose beauty must have impressed itself upon you as it has upon me (though not with the same results)—the likeness is not material, and I have seen nothing but Press pictures of my dream "Model".'

Plate 19. STATIONS OF THE DEAD*

Across the middle third of the canvas a vertical group of figures stands on the ground (one floating in the air), waiting as if in a queue. Their line is broken by upright rectangles of harsh white and shapes in other colours. At the feet of the two central figures, a wedge-shaped block in light, bright blue. Between the figures and the onlooker, in the lower third of the canvas, the floor of the cavern: black and brown with hints of red showing through the over-painting. Above the figures the cavern is pierced by a small cave mouth on the left-hand side and illuminated on the right by an irregular shaft of light descending vertically. A movement towards the left, above the figures, is created by the strata-lines of the rocks.

Oil on canvas. Size: 50 × 30½ *ins. Signed and dated lower left-hand corner, vertically: Wyndham Lewis* 1933 (Actually completed 1937).

Present owner: Mrs Naomi Mitchison.

Exhibited: Leicester Galleries, Wyndham Lewis exhibition, 1937, No. 53; also R.G.R.E., No. 119; also British Painting 1925-50, No. 36 (First Anthology), London and Manchester. (An Arts Council Exhibition, Festival of Britain, 1951.)

Plate 20. PLAYERS ON THE STAGE*

The four figures stand on the stage and, with it, fill the upper two-thirds of the canvas. Formalized curtains, catching a red glow, hang at the side and across the top of the proscenium. Encased in box-like costumes the figures might be sign-carriers in a modern ballet. The central figure is mechanistic, a Robot with a megaphone-mouth. The figure on the right inclines towards him; horns and ears show above his head. The two figures on the left lean away towards their own side of the stage, their backs towards us. One wears a mask designed like the head of a minotaur, the other supports a flat board with a heraldic device on it, the symbol of a head. The figures are painted in light colours: lemon yellow, bright blue, soft green, pale scarlet, orange. Below the stage, greatly reduced in size (in the lower third of the canvas), there is a reflection of the scene above. A fifth figure appears in the reflection bearing no relation to the figures above.

Oil on canvas. Size: 27 ×20 ins. Unsigned, undated (1937).
Present owners: The Leicester Galleries.
Exhibited: Leicester Galleries, Wyndham Lewis exhibition, 1937, No. 54; also R.G.R.E., No. 115.

Plate 21. THE MUD CLINIC*

A puce-coloured cylinder in the centre of the picture supports an upright, dummy-figure. In the top right-hand corner, an abstract scene of vertical, rectangular shapes in blacks and blues. To the left of the dummy-figure, three 'patients' lie horizontally. Behind them, a bright green tree against an emerald and sea-green background. Below the dummy, an area of broken, off-white shapes, partly obscured by the foreground figures; the two on the right of the canvas sitting against blocks of wood. Four or five heads and figures fill the lower left-hand corner of the canvas where the ground colour is yellow ochre.

Oil on canvas. Size: 33½×23¼ ins. Signed and dated lower left-hand corner, vertically: Wyndham Lewis 1937.
Present owner: The Artist.
Exhibited: Leicester Galleries, Wyndham Lewis exhibition 1937, No. 51; also R.G.R.E., No. 111.

Plate 22. INCA WITH BIRDS

In the foreground, three tall figures, two on the left, one on the right. The latter kneels on steps in the corner of the canvas, right side towards us, looking out of the picture. This figure is surrounded by a kind of echoing shape or penumbra. Very little can be seen of the figure on the extreme left, as it is on the edge of the canvas. The middle figure (the Inca) faces forward, ball-headed, swathed in leathery garments, his right arm raised above his head. All the figures are painted in varying tones of dark or hot red-brown. Between them, slightly to right of centre, a gap reveals a desert. The desert is sandy like the foreground (pale yellow touched with green) and recedes to the distance; where in the upper quarter of the picture a strip of water runs horizontally before a group of rectangular shapes, representing buildings. On the desert, near the centre of the picture, two birds. (See comment, p. 64.)

Oil on canvas. Size: untraced. Signed and dated, lower right-hand corner: Wyndham Lewis 1933.
Present owner: Mrs Lynette Roberts.
Reproduced: *The Pavilion*, edited by Myfanwy Evans, p. 12.
Exhibited: Leicester Galleries, Wyndham Lewis Exhibition, 1937, No. 42.

Plate 23. FOUR FIGURE COMPOSITION*

Four very tall female figures are ranged across the canvas at nearly equal distances. Of the two central figures, the one on the left sits on a tilted stool, well back in the picture space. The two figures on the right are a pair, the outer one a ghost or reflection of her partner; both, like the seated figured, are swathed in draperies. The three standing figurers are still, dignified; they wear tall head-dresses of feathers.

Behind the figures, on the left, a diagonal line composed of curious, rounded shapes. The whole group is arranged on a stage the edge of which forms a strong horizontal band receiving the vertical thrusts of the figures.

Oil on canvas. Size: unknown. Signed and dated lower left-hand corner: Wyndham Lewis 1938. Untraced. From a photograph in the possession of the artist.

Plate 24. ALLEGRESSE AQUATIQUE*

The strips of land in the background and foreground are arranged diagonally across the sheet, inclining down and left, the water running between them. Four abstracted figures on the near bank are linked with three in the water by an eighth figure standing between the two groups. An important feature of the design is the large cloud (nearly filling the upper half of the picture), the lower edge of which echoes, in reverse, the horizon curve of the land. Land and cloud are linked at one point by a building on the brow of the hill. Details of colour are not available.

Pen and black ink with washes in inks and water-colour. Size: $11\frac{3}{4} \times 16\frac{3}{4}$ ins. Signed and dated in ink, lower right-hand corner: Wyndham Lewis 1941.

Present owners: The Art Gallery of Toronto, Canada.

This is the only example here reproduced of the artist's work during his visit to Canada 1940–1948. Both with regard to subject-matter and composition the drawing is reminiscent of BEACH SCENE (Pl. 14, note p. 88.)

Plate 25. WHAT THE SEA IS LIKE AT NIGHT*

In the sky at the upper left-hand corner a white moon symbolizes night. A section of the sea, as though cut through a vast wave, reveals semi-human figures, fishes, oceanic life. The creatures swirling in the water give a strong diagonal movement to the design. Counter-rhythms break out near the surface of the water. The drawing is softened by thin paint, loosely controlled.

Colours: Pale yellow sky, peacock blues and greens in the water, also black and white shapes.

Pen and ink with water-colour washes: gouache. Size: $22 \times 14\frac{3}{4}$ ins., mounted. Signed and dated in ink, lower left-hand corner, vertically: Wyndham Lewis 1949.

Present owners: Mr and Mrs W. Doge Hutchinson.

Provenance: The Redfern Gallery.

Exhibited: R.G.R.E., No. 46.

The artist says of this picture that '. . . in the greatly stylized image of the ocean, semi-human animals plunge and obtrude themselves as if they had found their way into this from another dimension.' (From a letter to the Editor, September, 1950.)

Plate 26. A BATTERY SHELLED

The design of this very large picture (approximately 6×10 ft.) is full and complex. In the left foreground three Army officers stand in a group, with equipment, in front of a concrete and steel structure connected with guns. In the right foreground, a group of shattered tree stumps. In the middle of the picture, at a lower level, an area of muddy ground, stiff and corrugated, where numerous formalized figures are at work. Enclosing the area of corrugated ground, several gun emplacements with, here and there, shell dumps, camouflage nets, shelter entrances, etc. Over the whole scene, across the pale sky in the upper third of the picture, and moving from left to right, strong and angular spurts of smoke.

At the time of writing it is still not possible to inspect this picture and in consequence details of colour are not available.

Oil on canvas. Size: 72×125 ins. Signed and dated at the left-hand edge of the canvas, about 18 inches from the base: WL 19 (1919).

Present owners: The Imperial War Museum, London.

Reproduced: *The Studio*, vol. 118, p. 232.

For Mr Newton's discussion of this picture, see p. 21. There is a related work in the same collection, perhaps one of numerous studies from which the picture was ultimately painted:

A BATTERY POSITION IN A WOOD

In this drawing the same subjects are introduced—shelter entrances, tree stumps, shell dumps, gun emplacements—but they are differently disposed.

Pen and ink, crayon and water-colour washes. Size: 12½ × 18½ ins. Signed and dated in ink, lower right-hand corner: Wyndham Lewis 1918.

A large oil painting in the National Gallery of Art, Ottawa, is in many ways similar to the BATTERY SHELLED, above:

A CANADIAN GUNPIT

In this close-up of a gunpit the details of the gun itself, the overhanging camouflage nets, and the groups of very large shells are all clearly drawn and painted. It is even larger than the example in the Imperial War Museum (measuring approximately 10 × 11 ft.). The figures are in the act of laying the gun.

Oil on canvas. Size: 121¼ × 132 ins. Unsigned, undated (1918).

Reproduced: Konody, *Art and War*, in colour, Pl. 35 (Canadian War Memorials, ?1918). Exhibited: London; New York, Anderson Galleries; Toronto, Canadian War Memorials, 1919, No. 66; Ottawa, National Gallery, Second Exhibition of Canadian War Memorials, 1924, No. 47; New York, Museum of Modern Art, etc.

A sketch for A CANADIAN GUNPIT, 14 × 20 ins., with the same title, is in the same collection.

Plate 27. RED NUDE*

The model stands with her back towards the onlooker, arms folded, her right side slightly nearer to us than the left. Swiftly drawn pencil lines are washed over in tones of dark red, brown and green water-colour. In this typical example of the life drawings of this year the model's hair is represented by outline only.

Pencil and water-colour washes. Size: 22¼ × 16¼ ins. Signed and dated in ink, lower left-hand corner: Wyndham Lewis 1919.

Present owners: The British Council.

Exhibited: R.G.R.E., No. 31; also at the 'Exhibition of Contemporary British Art", No. 61, when the New Burlington Galleries were reopened in November 1949.

For further details of the life drawing of this year, see p. 67.

Plate 28. GIRL IN A WINDSOR CHAIR*

The model sits in the chair facing slightly to the right. The pose is easy, the figure and chair make a compact group. The hair is thick, heavily drawn, the face put in with very few lines. Jacket and skirt are voluminous, loose fitting; the drawing is a life study with the emphasis on the treatment of the drapery. The hands are suppressed, though the feet are more fully drawn than usual.

Chalk. Size: 21 × 14½ ins. Signed and dated in ink, lower left-hand corner: Wyndham Lewis 1920.

Present owners: Rutherston Collection.

Exhibited: R.G.R.E., No. 74.

The same collection includes nine other drawings from this year, six of which were exhibited at the R.G.R.E. For Mr Newton's discussion of this drawing, see p. 22; p. 68 for other comments. The chair is a 'property' of the period.

Plate 29. GIRL LOOKING DOWN* (Sketch of Mary Webb)

In this head and shoulders study the novelist looks down and shows the left side of her face. Falling hair obscures the eyes. The interior modelling of the face is carefully drawn and shaded, the outline emphasizes the rounded contour curves.

Pencil. Size: 11⅜×14⅜ ins., mounted. Signed and dated in ink, lower right-hand corner: W. Lewis 1919.

Present owner: Wyndham T. Vint, Esq.

Exhibited: R.G.R.E., No. 63.

Plate 30. STUDY OF AN ELDERLY MAN*

In this head and shoulders study the model's left hand is raised to support his face. Face, hand and the upper part of jacket and waistcoat (like the details of shirt, collar, tie, etc.) are heavily worked in great detail. The firm, deliberate draughtsmanship, dark with wash and cross-hatching, emphasizes the absence of the eyes.

Conté crayon and pen and ink washes with water. Size: unknown. Signed and dated in ink, lower right-hand corner: Wyndham Lewis 1920. (The double line over 'Lewis' is a characteristic of the signature during the early twenties.) Untraced. From a photograph in the possession of the artist.

This is probably a study of the London 'Cabby' who was a favourite model of the period and of whom numerous drawings were made. Other examples include:

LONDON CABBY

In this drawing the model wears the heavy cabman's coat well wrapped round his body. He sits in a chair facing the onlooker, hands sunk deep in his pockets. Brown washes on the face, with a green wash on the scarf round his neck. The heavy moustache helps to identify the sitter.

Pencil, crayon and water-colour washes. Size: 14⅜×11 3/16 ins., mounted. Signed and dated in pencil, lower right-hand corner: Wyndham Lewis 1920.

Present owner: Arthur Crossland, Esq.

Exhibited: R.G.R.E., No. 87.

Plate 31. WOMAN WITH CLASPED HANDS*

The model sits on a high stool, facing the onlooker, the upper part of her body inclining slightly forward and left. Her hands are lightly clasped and rest on the corner of the card table which is arranged at an angle and covered with paper or a cloth.

Pencil. Size: 10⅞×10½ ins. Signed and dated in ink, lower right-hand corner: Wyndhand Lewis 1921.

Present owners: Rutherston Collection.

Exhibited: R.G.R.E., No. 78.

The striped cuffs, full skirt, sleeveless jacket and the card table all reappear in other drawings of the period. For further details see p. 68; also Pls. 32, 33, and the Notes below. Details of the following example, also mentioned on p. 68, are here relevant:

WOMAN WITH RED TAM O' SHANTER

Pencil, pen and ink and water-colour washes. Size: 15⅛×18¾ ins., mounted. Signed and dated in ink, lower left-hand corner: Wyndham Lewis 1921.

Present owners: Michael Cartwright Sharp and Charles Handley-Read.

Exhibited: R.G.R.E., No. 1. Reproduced in the catalogue.

Plate 32. SEATED FIGURE

The model sits in a slightly hunched position at the edge of an armchair, the latter partially indicated in very faint lines. We see a full three-quarter view of face and figure. An outline drawing in which the face and hands only are modelled with shading. The two-buttoned link of the jacket, the arrangement of the hair and the heavy eyebrows are all typical of the period.

Probably conté crayon. Size: unknown. Unsigned, undated (1921). Untraced. From a photograph in the possession of the artist.
Reproduced: *Wyndham Lewis the Artist: from Blast to Burlington House*, opposite p. 112

Plate 33. GIRL SEWING*

The model sits on the edge of the table, crouched over her sewing, her right foot just touching the floor. We see her at an angle from the left-hand side. Much of the figure is heavily shaded to produce the effect of grey washes; but the jacket, the left hand and the face (the latter largely obscured by the tam o' shanter), also the treatment of the sleeve, are all features common to numerous examples of the artist's life studies of the period.
Conté crayon. Size: unknown. Unsigned, undated (1921). Untraced. From a photograph in the possession of the artist.

Plate 34. MRS DESMOND HARMSWORTH

As in most examples of the 'Thirty Personalities' series, this is a head-and-shoulders portrait-drawing, but with rather more than usual emphasis on the hands, here intricately locked together and held up beneath the chin. The dark shading across the shoulder line and at the base of the neck in this example are also features of the series. Typical of the artist's style are the familiar petal-shapes in the drawing of the hair and the sharply articulated points of the jabot. (Numerous examples, as here, show considerable emphasis of cuffs and collars, both in the male and female portrait drawings.) Notable also is the spontaneous line, uncorrected by the use of a rubber; and the shading round the eyes which give the face the appearance of being carved or moulded.
Pencil. Size: unknown. Signed and dated in pencil at the base of the drawing, left: Wyndham Lewis 1932. From a photograph of the plate in the publication (see note p. 43).
Present owner: Desmond Harmsworth, Esq.
Exhibited: The Lefevre Galleries, 'Thirty Personalities' Exhibition, 1932.
The portraits of the late DUNCAN MACDONALD and of MISS MARIE NEY in the above series, both in the possession of Mrs Duncan Macdonald, were exhibited during 1949 at the City Museum and Art Gallery, Birmingham.
The portrait of WING COMMANDER ORLEBAR is in the possession of Temple Newsam House, Leeds. This drawing, together with six other examples from the same series, was reproduced in *The Studio*, vol. 104, pp. 262-268.
The portrait of J. B. PRIESTLEY is in the possession of the Graves Art Gallery, Sheffield. Most of the portraits in the series are privately owned.

Plate 35. THE CHAIN SMOKER*

A rapid pencil sketch. The model leans back against the sofa (note the waving-line pattern), her left arm raised, her right arm resting on a cushion and poised, from ths elbow up, in the air. She wears a wide-brimmed hat and in her right hand she hold, a cigarette. Face and hands are characteristically drawn in sharp, spontaneous lines both washed with pale yellow. Very interesting shadows are assembled round the base of the nose. The intensity of the gaze from the luminous eyes, looking straight towards the observer, is in contrast to the languid pose.
Pencil and water-colour wash. Size: $11\frac{3}{4} \times 15\frac{1}{4}$ ins. Signed and dated in pencil, lower left-hand corner of drawing: W. Lewis 1935.
Present owner: Charles Handley-Read, Esq.
Provenance: The Leicester Galleries.
Exhibited: Leicester Galleries, Wyndham Lewis exhibition, 1937, probably No. 12

NOTES ON THE PLATES

Plate 36. PORTRAIT OF MRS T. J. HONEYMAN*

Seated with legs crossed, hands folded in her lap, the sitter is turned slightly away from the onlooker for a rather more than three-quarter view. She wears a brightly coloured evening jacket and long satin evening skirt. On the left, level with the back of the chair, a passage of abstracted decoration again in bright colours.

Colours: Face, arms and hands, soft flesh tones; hair deep auburn. Jacket yellow and black, the skirt old gold. The upholstery of the chair in pink-toned beige, the drapery over the arm of the chair in pink-grey. The wall background in green-blue, light in tone, the abstracted decoration in browns and greens, and the floor in dark blue-grey.

Oil on canvas. Size: 30 × 20 *ins. Signed (undated), lower right-hand corner: Wyndham Lewis* (1936 *or* 1937).

Present owner: T. J. Honeyman, Esq.

Plate 37. PORTRAIT OF MISS EDITH SITWELL

The figure sits upright in the arm-chair, body three-quarters left, head erect and facing front, the eyes cast down, hands buried in the scarf on the lap. Figure and chair are placed to the right of the canvas, backed by several vertical panels, a screen and, upper left, a curtain. To the left, books on a shelf and the seat of a chair covered in striped upholstery; also various near-abstract shapes. Lower right-hand corner, a globe on a stand.

Colours: A yellow skirt and green jacket, bright reds and blues in the scarf. The chair and all other details in various shades of brown, except for the panels of blue and the red-brown curtain, all in the background.

Oil on canvas. Size: 34 × 44 *ins. Signed (undated) lower left-hand corner: Wyndham Lewis.* (*Begun* 1923, *completed* 1935.)

Present owners: The Tate Gallery, No. 5437. Purchased out of the Knapping Fund, 1943.

Reproduced: *The Studio*, May 1944, vol. 127, in colour, p. 148.

Plate 38. WOMAN IN AN ARMCHAIR

The model sits back in the armchair, eyes closed, her left arm raised, thumbs and little-finger-tips lightly touching. Firelight from the left casts a warm, golden glow on the face and sleeves, creates sharp but delicate shadows on the face, hair and raised arm. The clear and delicate lines of the face, hands and sleeve are in contrast to the loose infilling of parts of the blouse. The effect of firelight is produced by the economical use of a gold-yellow wash. A touch of deep purple shadow on the lap.

Pencil and water-colour washes. Size: 12 × 15 *ins. Signed and dated in pencil, lower right-hand corner of drawing: Wyndham Lewis* 1936.

Present owner: Charles Handley-Read, Esq.

Provenance: Redfern Gallery.

Exhibited: R.G.R.E. No. 9. Reproduced in the catalogue.

This drawing is typical of the life studies of the period and shows the blouse and cuffs often seen in other examples (as in PORTRAIT DRAWING OF THE ARTIST'S WIFE, Pl. 39, note p. 97). The eyebrow lines, and the shading round the eyes, show the precise shapes of a cornice-moulding (see p. 69 for further discussion of this point). Numerous related drawings include:

READING

In this drawing the model sits on the far side of a table, to the right, looking down at a book held in her left hand. The right hand supports the chin. She wears a blouse with 'bishop' sleeves and tight cuffs as in the above example. Several tones of warm yellow-brown wash are added to the delicate draughtsmanship and careful shading.

Pencil and water-colour wash. Size: 13$\frac{5}{16}$ ×9$\frac{7}{8}$ *ins., mounted. Signed and dated in pencil, lower right-hand corner: Wyndham Lewis 1936.*
Present owners: The British Museum. Acquired through the Contemporary Art Society, 1939.
Reproduced: *From Sickert to 1948*, Lund Humphries, 1948, Pl. No. 57.

YOUNG WOMAN SEATED
In this drawing the model sits in an arm-chair, facing the onlooker, but with body at three-quarter view. Her right arm is raised on the arm of the chair, her left placed across the body. Full sleeves and tight cuffs, as above. Yellow and red-brown washes.
Pencil and water-colour washes. Size: 15×11 *ins., mounted. Signed and dated in pencil, lower right-hand corner: Wyndham Lewis 1936.*
Present owner: Michael Ayrton, Esq.
Reproduced: *The Studio*, vol. 132, p. 105 (as STUDY OF A WOMAN).
Exhibited: R.G.R.E., No. 93.

Plate 39. PORTRAIT DRAWING OF THE ARTIST'S WIFE

The sitter is posed to show a three-quarter view of the face and upper part of the body, the left shoulder dropping down, the left arm resting horizontally along the knee. Her right arm indicates that the invisible hand rests on her hip. In the drawing of the head, the emphasis is on the large eyes; and on the hair and ear. The passages to be shaded are selected with deliberation, and applied with economy, to assist the design of the whole drawing. Note the full sleeves and tight cuffs of the period.
Conté crayon. Size: 13×10$\frac{1}{8}$ *ins., mounted. Signed and dated in pencil, lower right-hand corner: Wyndham Lewis 1936.*
Present owner: the Artist.
Reproduced: *The Studio*, vol. 115, p. 154.
Exhibited: Leicester Galleries, Wyndham Lewis Exhibition, 1937, No. 3, as STUDY OF A YOUNG WOMAN.

Plate 40. PORTRAIT OF T. S. ELIOT (1938)

The sitter is posed so that we look squarely at him, his head and eyes inclined very slightly down and left. The onlooker's eye is on a level with the sitter's hands, hence the foreshortening of the thighs. Figure and chair are placed on the vertical axis of the canvas. The flat background, immediately behind the chair, is made up of a wide central panel on which is cast a shadow of the head. This panel is flanked on either side by narrow strips in the same plane decorated with abstracted patterns. As Mr Newton remarks, the general shape of the figure resembles a crossbow (see p. 30). Colours: Face and hands in sun-burnt flesh tones. The suit in shades of blue, blue-green. The upholstery of the chair in dull apricot, the woodwork in ochre. The central panel behind the figure in very pale leaf green, the richly decorated side panels, chiefly in black and brown, are touched with red, purple, etc. Behind and below the figure the panel on the right side changes to soft, dull blue in the lower corner of the picture.
Oil on canvas. Size: 52×33$\frac{1}{2}$ *ins. Signed (undated) lower right-hand corner: Wyndham Lewis (1938).*
Present owners: Durban Municipal Art Gallery, South Africa.
Exhibited: Beaux Arts Gallery, Exhibition of New Paintings and Drawings by Wyndham Lewis, Summer, 1938, No. 10.
Reproduced: In the Press and numerous journals in 1938; also *Wyndham Lewis the Artist: from Blast to Burlington House*, in colour, frontispiece; also in *Time*, vol. 53, May 30, 1949, p. 60 (together with a reproduction of the 1949 portrait, Pl. B, note p. 82). It was the rejection of this portrait from exhibition at the Royal Academy in 1938

that prompted the resignation, for two years, of Augustus John. An account of the incident is given in *Wyndham Lewis the Artist: from Blast to Burlington House*, pp. 373–380.

Plate 41. THE RED PORTRAIT*

The figure sits in a light armchair, looking left, showing a full three-quarter view of the face. Her left hand rests in her lap, the upraised right hand holds a cigarette. Behind the figure a fireplace with, in the lower right-hand corner, a fire; also an over-mantel with a painted scene and a brass ornament. To the left, a standard lamp and a bookcase.

Colours: Predominantly red-brown tones, heightened to orange in the fire. Various blues in the fireplace and on the lamp-shade and standard. The face and hands picked out in highlights of very pale flesh tones. A portrait of the artist's wife in which the full sleeves and tight cuffs, seen in Pls. 38 and 39, and in READING and YOUNG WOMAN SEATED (quoted on pp. 96 and 97, respectively), again appear.

Oil on canvas. Size: 36 × 24 ins. Signed and dated, lower right-hand corner: Wyndham Lewis 1937.

Present owner: Mrs Eva Handley-Read.

Provenance: The Zwemmer Gallery.

Exhibited: R.G.R.E., No. 124.

The title was chosen deliberately by the artist to emphasize the fact of the figure being worked up from the red tones it shares with the background. For further remarks about this picture, see p. 72.

Plate 42. PORTRAIT OF STEPHEN SPENDER*

The sitter's pose resembles that of Mr T. S. Eliot in the 'first' portrait, but the view-point is much closer. The onlooker's eye is level with the sitter's head. The chair is pushed against the wall on which there are sections of two abstractions. In the upper right-hand corner, a bookcase. The face is worked in fat, smooth paint.

Colours: Face and hands in very strong red-brown. The trousers in grey-green; the shirt in clear, light blue—a dominant feature of the painting. The upholstery of the chair in light pink brown; and the wall behind the sitter in very pale light yellow.

Oil on canvas. Size: 39½ × 23¼ ins. Signed and dated, lower left-hand corner: Wyndham Lewis 1938.

Present owners: Public Museum and Art Gallery, Hanley.

Exhibited: Beaux Arts Gallery, Exhibition of New Paintings and Drawings by Wyndham Lewis, 1938, No. 1; also R.G.R.E., No. 128; also British Painting 1925-50, No. 37 (First Anthology), London and Manchester. (An Arts Council Exhibition, Festival of Britain, 1951.)

Plate 43. PORTRAIT OF MRS NAOMI MITCHISON*

The sitter leans forward in the chair, her left arm raised so that the chin rests on her hand, the elbow on the open book. The book in turn supports the right hand. A close three-quarter view showing the left side of the face, the onlooker's eyes on a level with the head. On the table, left, an open file-box and an ash-tray.

Colours: Face and hands in light flesh tones, the hair dark brown, the frock dark blue with white collars and cuffs. A light background in a neutral shade. The chair dark brown, the sketch painting of the crucifixion picked out in bright flame colour. The curtain, top right, in orange-scarlet.

Oil on canvas. Size: 40 × 30 ins. Signed (undated) lower left-hand corner: Wyndham Lewis (1938).

Present owner: Mrs Naomi Mitchison.

Exhibited: R.G.R.E. No. 113.

NOTES ON THE PLATES

Plate 44. PORTRAIT DRAWING OF AVRION, SON OF MRS MITCHISON*

The boy shows the right side of his face, three-quarter view. His closed eyes suggest determination to hold the position for a strictly limited period. This nearly life-size drawing is one of a small series made of the sons of Mrs Mitchison, all commissioned at the same time. It is one of the artist's very few child-studies.

Black conté crayon. Size: 15¾×13 *ins. Signed and dated in conté, centrally, below the drawing: Wyndham Lewis* 1938.

Present owner: Mrs Naomi Mitchison.

Plate 45. LYNETTE*

Seen from the three-quarter view, with her knees crossed, the figure is placed diagonally across the sheet, her left side nearest the onlooker. Her arms hang by her side, the left hand lightly gripping the seat of the chair. The head inclines down and left. Very dark shading is applied to the folds of the long skirt, to the neck below the chin, on the hair and at the left elbow.

Conté crayon. Size: 15×11 *ins. Signed and dated in conté crayon, lower right-hand corner: Wyndham Lewis* 1948.

Present owner: the Artist.

With its heavy shading and delicate modelling (here and there softened by finger-smudges) this drawing is typical of many life studies made during recent years. The emphasis on form rather than on line indicates an interesting contrast between present technique and the technique seen in many earlier examples.

Plate 46. HEAD OF EZRA POUND* (Sketch)

A vigorous drawing of the poet's head, facing right, a study for the portrait in the Tate Gallery of the same year (Pl. 47, note p. 100).

Conté crayon. Size: 13×10 *ins., mounted. Signed and dated in pencil, left of centre at the base of the drawing: Wyndham Lewis* 1938.

Present owner: Wyndham T. Vint, Esq.

Exhibited: R.G.R.E. No.· 62.

Numerous sketches of Ezra Pound include three further examples exhibited at the R.G.R.E.:

1. EZRA POUND SEATED

In this drawing the poet sits in an armchair, facing the observer, one hand on the lapel of his jacket, his right leg stretched forward.·

Black chalk. Size: 14⅜×12⅞ *ins., mounted. Signed, dated and inscribed, lower right-hand corner, in chalk: Wyndham Lewis* 1921. *Drawing of Ezra Pound.*

Present owners: The Redfern Gallery.

Exhibited: R.G.R.E. No. 39.

2. EZRA POUND

In this drawing we see the left side of the head in profile. The head is placed in the upper right-hand corner of the sheet. The poet looks down.

Chalk. Size: 14¾×13¼ *ins., mounted. Signed (undated) and inscribed in ink, lower left-hand corner: Drawing of Ezra Pound by Wyndham Lewis* (1921).

Present owner: The Redfern Gallery.

Exhibited: R.G.R.E., No. 69.

3. POET SEATED, EZRA POUND

In this drawing the poet is again seated in an armchair, both hands on the lapels of his jacket, facing slightly left, both legs stretched out in line with the direction of his gaze.

Crayon. Size: 14¾×19 *ins. Signed (undated) in ink, lower right-hand corner: Wyndham Lewis* (1921).

Present owners: Rutherston Collection.
Exhibited: R.G.R.E. No. 69.

Plate 47. PORTRAIT OF EZRA POUND

The poet sits back in the armchair showing the left side of his face, eyes closed relaxed. His head is in the upper right-hand corner of the canvas and in line with the diagonal of the body. Beside him, a table with a newspaper and three ash-trays. In the background a lightly painted canvas leans against the wall. An architectural moulding appears in the upper left-hand corner of the canvas.

Colours: Face and hands hot, ruddy brown: hair and beard, chestnut. The jacket black (very thinly painted, showing canvas), with a pale green shirt and hot brown tie deeply shaded in black. Background very pale green, floor dark brown, table mid-brown, newspaper shaded in light grey.

Oil on canvas. Size: 30 ×40 *ins. Unsigned, undated* (1938).

Present owners: The Tate Gallery, No. 5042. Purchased out of the Knapping Fund, 1939.

Reproduced: *Picture Post*, March 1939, in colour, illustrating an article by Dr John Rothenstein (see previous note, p. 89).

For further details of this picture, see p. 72; also the preliminary sketch for the head (in reverse) Pl. 46, note p. 99.

The following details of one of the complete and final studies for the above portrait are here relevant:

STUDY FOR THE PORTRAIT OF EZRA POUND

In this water-colour drawing the artist has tried out the arrangement, finally adopted, of the figure placed diagonally across the picture space. The pose in this study and in the Tate Gallery portrait are the same. The table and glass ash-tray also appear in the study, though not the newspaper nor the picture canvas in the background.

The drawing is very delicately painted as follows: face and hands, pale pink; hair and beard, light auburn; coat and chair-arms, light yellow. Hints of pale blue-green appear on the shirt, tie and ash-tray.

Pencil and water-colour washes. Size: 14¾ ×21 *ins., mounted. Colour of paper: light buff. Signed and dated at an angle, in black chalk, lower left-hand corner: Wyndham Lewis* 1938.

Present owner: the Artist.

Plate 48. PORTRAIT OF JOHN MACLEOD*

The sitter has sunk down in the armchair, one leg raised so that his left knee supports his left hand, the other leg stretched out and across the base of the canvas. The sitter's eye is on a level with the head. The portrait is painted from a very close view-point.

Colours: Very warm brown-pink flesh tones on face and hands. The suit silver grey, with a soft blue shirt and dark green tie. Blue-green tones in the chair. A soft yellow on the wall behind the chair, grey browns in the picture on the wall. (Here the artist was working from a photograph of a Berber Palace pinned up to form part of the background.)

Oil on canvas. Size: 30 ×20 *ins. Signed and dated lower left-hand corner: Wyndham Lewis* 1938.

Present owner: The Artist.
Exhibited: R.G.R.E. No. 109.

INDEX

Note:—Titles of drawings and paintings are entered in small capitals. Entries in italics refer to the published works of Wyndham Lewis. Extracts from these works, whether chapters, essays, poems or manifestos, are in roman type and with quotation marks. Other literary or artistic publications are also in italics but the name of the author, editor or publisher follows the title in each case. Subjects of portraits are listed by surname.

INDEX

INDEX

INDEX

INDEX

Plates

1. TWO FIGURES (1912)

2. MAN AND WOMAN (1912)

5. A DESIGN FOR THE PUBLICATION *TIMON OF ATHENS*
(1913 or 1914)

4. PLANNERS (1913)

5. THE CENTAURESS (1912)

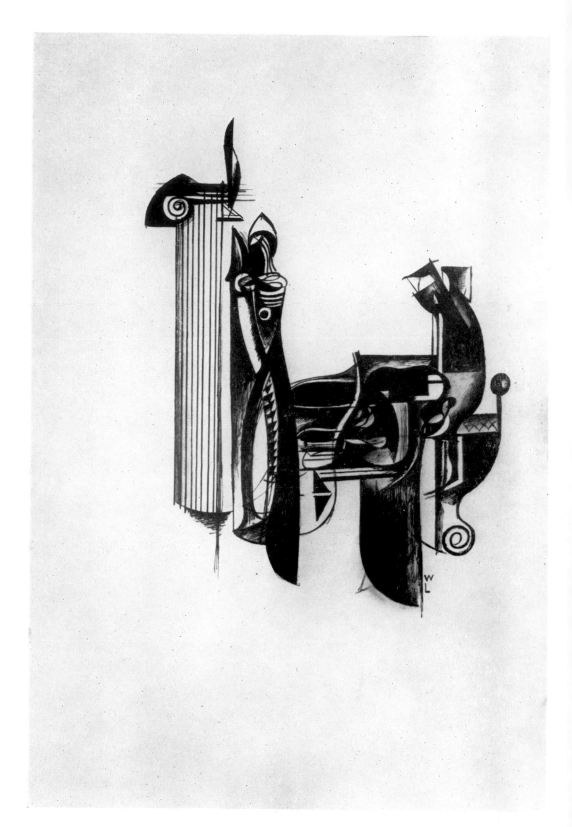

6. THE PILLAR (1927)

7. BIRD AND FIGURE (1925)

8. SENTINELS (1928)

9. BAGDAD: A PANEL (1927)

10. ATHANATON (1933)

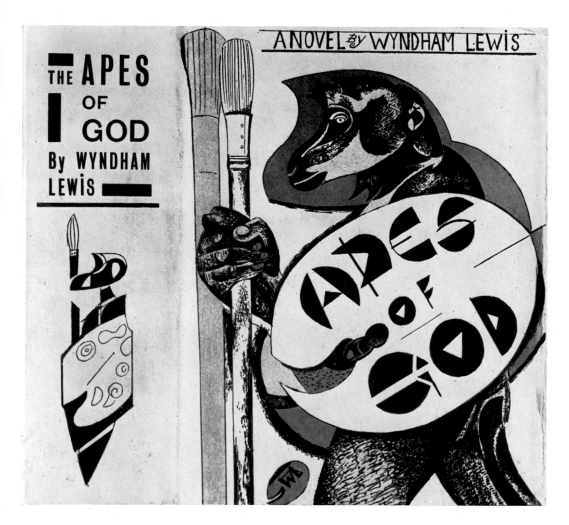

11. DUST WRAPPER FOR *THE APES OF GOD* (1929)

12. MONKS (1934)

13. BEACH BABIES (completed 1936)

14. BEACH SCENE (c. 1929)

15. ROMAN ACTORS (1934)

16. SURRENDER OF BARCELONA (1936)
(By courtesy of the Trustees of the Tate Gallery)

17. THE ARMADA (1937)

18. DEPARTURE OF A PRINCESS FROM CHAOS (1937)

19. STATIONS OF THE DEAD (completed 1937)

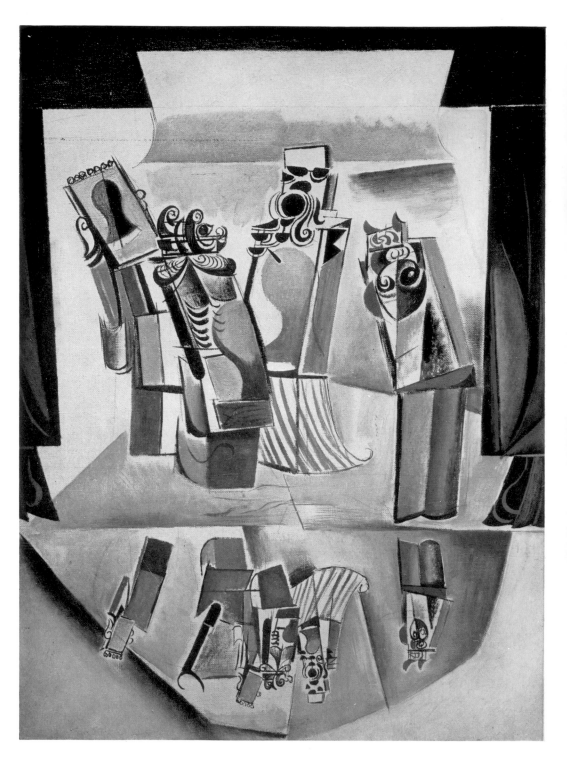

20. PLAYERS ON THE STAGE (1937)

21. THE MUD CLINIC (1937)

22. INCA WITH BIRDS (1933)

23. FOUR FIGURE COMPOSITION (1938)

24. ALLEGRESSE AQUATIQUE (1941)

25. WHAT THE SEA IS LIKE AT NIGHT (1949)

26. A BATTERY SHELLED (1919)

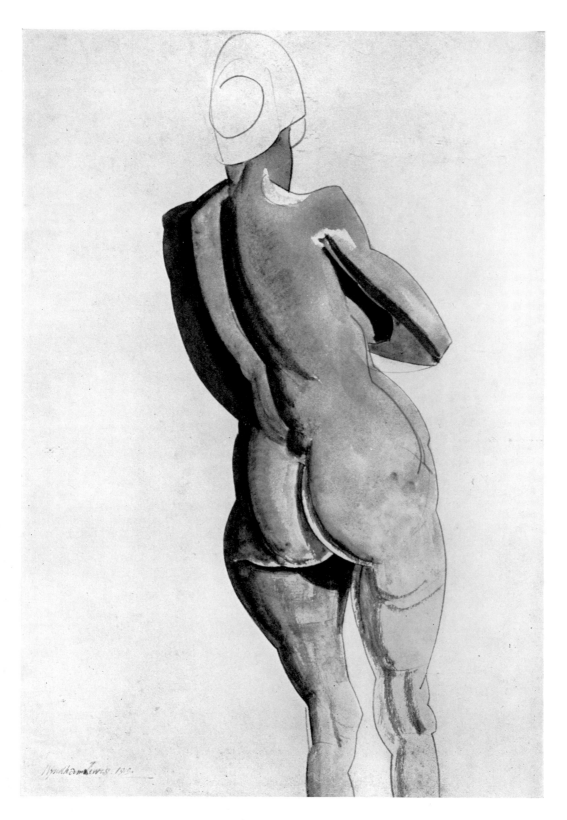

27. RED NUDE (1919)

28. GIRL IN A WINDSOR CHAIR (1920)

29. GIRL LOOKING DOWN (Sketch of Mary Webb) (1919)

30. STUDY OF AN ELDERLY MAN (1920)

31. WOMAN WITH CLASPED HANDS (1921)

32. SEATED FIGURE (1921)

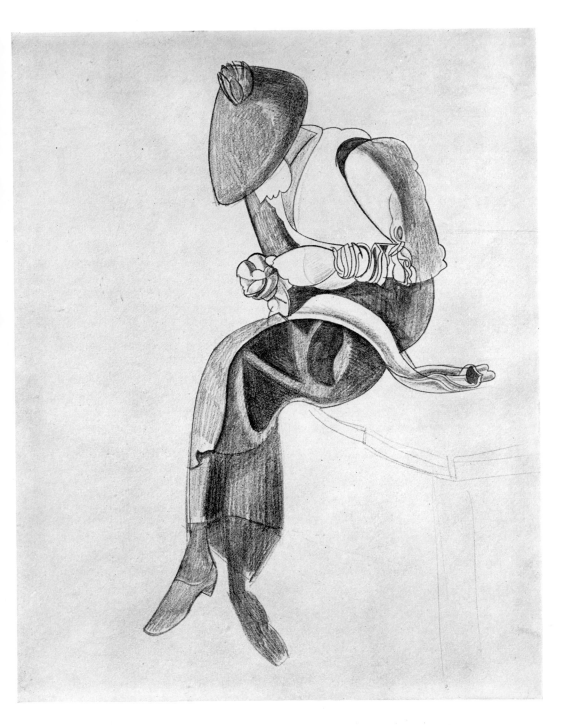

33. GIRL SEWING (1921)

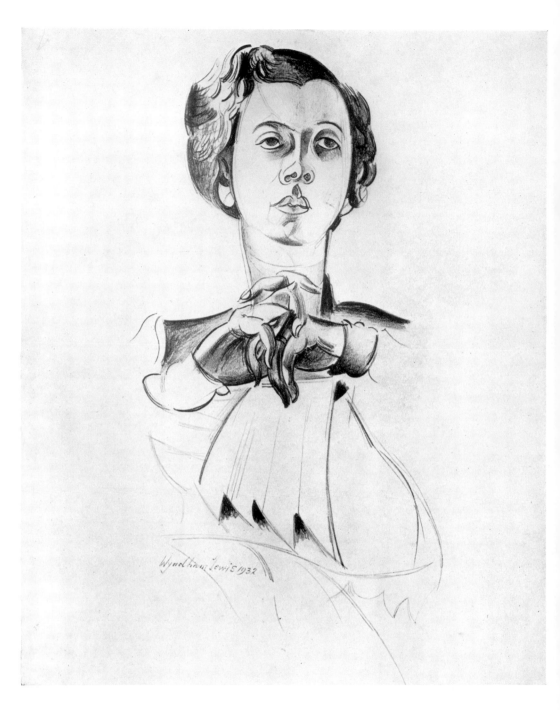

34. MRS DESMOND HARMSWORTH (1932)

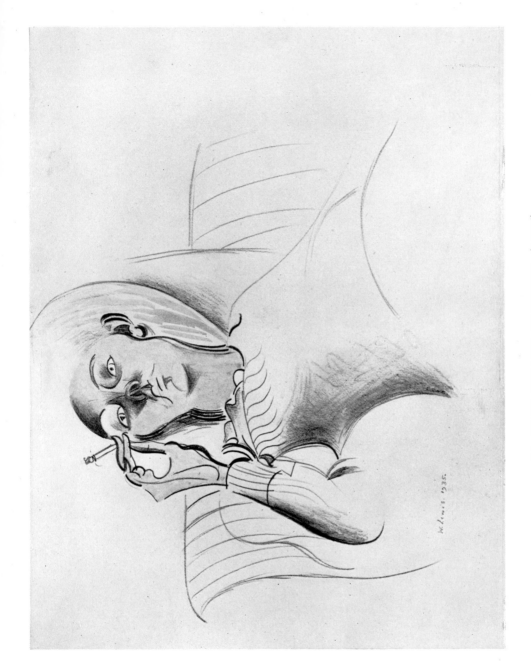

55. THE CHAIN SMOKER (1935)

36. PORTRAIT OF MRS T. J. HONEYMAN (1936 or 1937)

37. PORTRAIT OF MISS EDITH SITWELL (begun 1923, completed 1935)
By courtesy of the Trustees of the Tate Gallery

38. WOMAN IN AN ARMCHAIR (1936)

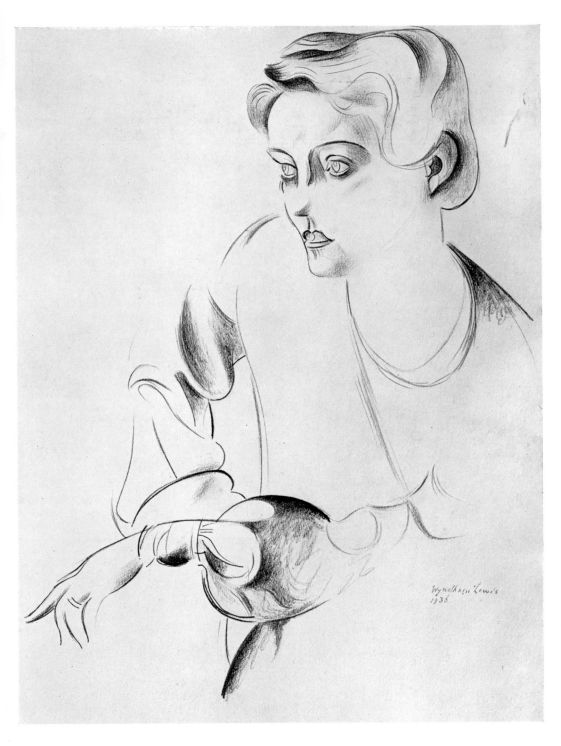

39. PORTRAIT DRAWING OF THE ARTIST'S WIFE (1936)

40. PORTRAIT OF T. S. ELIOT (1938)

41. THE RED PORTRAIT (1937)

42. PORTRAIT OF STEPHEN SPENDER (1938)

43. PORTRAIT OF MRS NAOMI MITCHISON (1938)

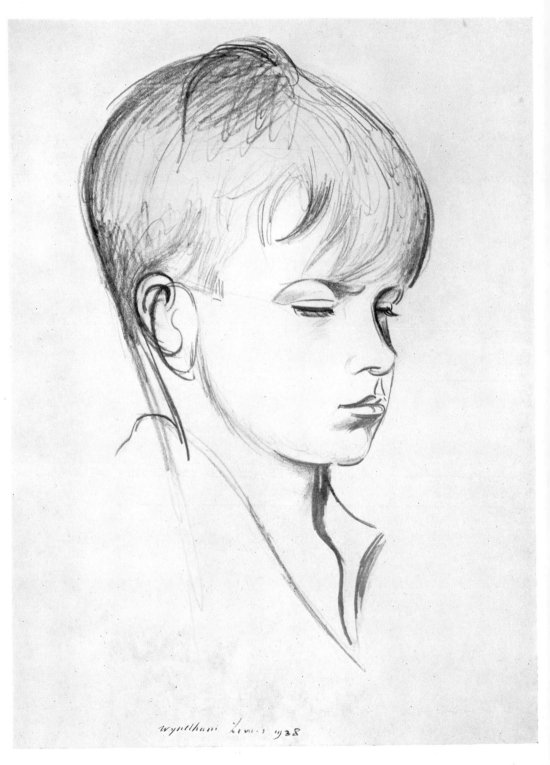

Wyndham Lewis 1938

44. PORTRAIT DRAWING OF AVRION, SON OF MRS MITCHISON (1938)

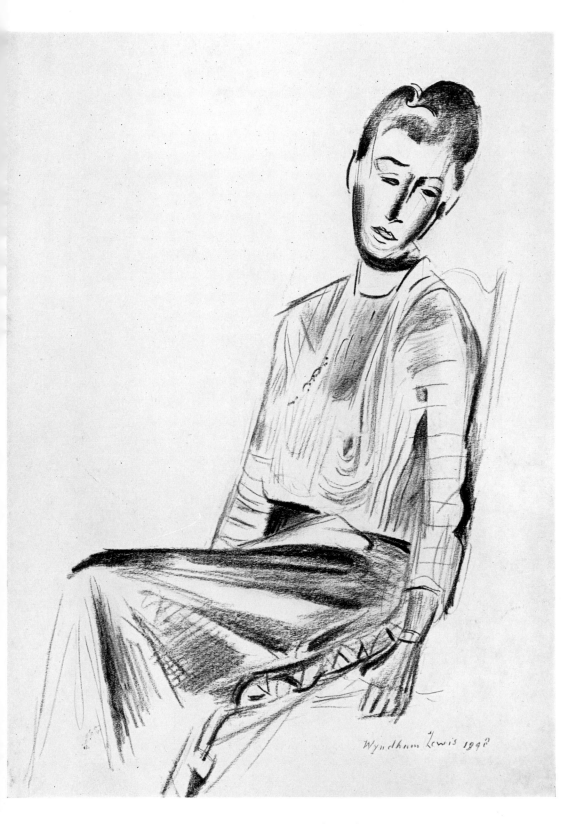

45. LYNETTE (1948)

46. HEAD OF EZRA POUND (Sketch) (1938)

47. PORTRAIT OF EZRA POUND (1938)
By courtesy of the Trustees of the Tate Gallery

48. PORTRAIT OF JOHN MACLEOD (1938)